SECRETS

OF THE SECRET PLACE

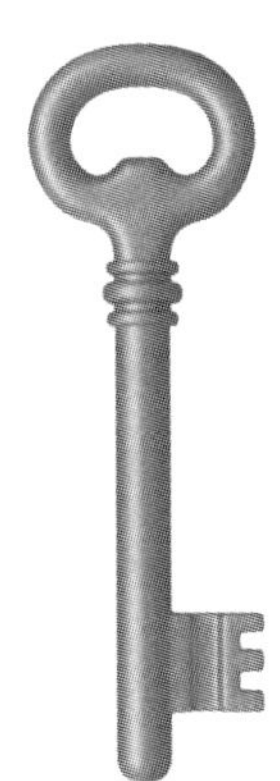

BOB SORGE

LEGACY EDITION

Oasis House, Kansas City, Missouri

First Hardcover Printing (2021)

(Also available in several languages, visit www.oasishouse.com for a current listing)

For information on all Bob's books, see page 222.

SECRETS OF THE SECRET PLACE
 Published by Oasis House
PO Box 522
Grandview, MO 64030-0522

www.oasishouse.com

Cover design: Andrew Chen

Printed in the United States of America

International Standard Book Number: 978-1-937725-56-3

Library of Congress Cataloging-in-Publication Data

Sorge, Bob.
Secrets of the secret place / Bob Sorge.
p.cm.
ISBN 978-1-937725-56-3 (hbk.)
1. Prayer—Christianity—Meditations. I. Title.

BV210.3 S67 2001
242'.2—dc21 2001035441

Stay connected please at:
YouTube.com/Bobsorge
Instagram: bob.sorge
Store: www.oasishouse.com
Blog: bobsorge.com
twitter.com/BOBSORGE
Facebook.com/BobSorgeMinistry

This book, by my friend Bob Sorge, sits on my Classics shelf alongside just a few other titles. It should be mandatory for every disciple of Jesus who hungers for greater intimacy with the Father. The book you're holding carries sheer revelation. Be refreshed from dry, religious obligation. I can't recommend it enough.

Lee M. Cummings, Senior Leader, Radiant Church,
Kalamazoo, Michigan, and author, *Flourish*

It is no secret what God wants most—for His children to pursue Him radically. What has remained a secret, however, is how to sustain the lifestyle of a fiery heart. Bob gives us a roadmap for navigating through the distractions. The secret is out! Learn how to get there and stay there.

Travis Greene, Recording Artist and Pastor,
Forward City Church, Columbia, South Carolina

My copy of this book is well-worn. I re-read it every few years, and often pass copies to hungry friends. Timeless and fresh, the message within these pages brings life to my insides as I see Him, seeing me, in secret.

Sara Hagerty, author,
Adore, and *Every Bitter Thing is Sweet*

Nothing rivals the importance of living in the secret place of the Most High. But how do we discover its beauty and life-transforming power? How do we overcome the constant distractions of our wired world and learn to stay in the secret place? In this readable and inspirational book, Bob Sorge shows us the way.

Dr. Michael L. Brown, President,
FIRE School of Ministry

Bob Sorge is one of my all-time favorite authors. His books don't just minister to the soul but feed the spirit. Forged on the anvil of suffering, he speaks through the tip of his pen. This book is the capstone of the message he's been given for the body of Christ. Every secret Bob reveals is like a tether that draws me back to my secret place—where I'm happiest.

John Kilpatrick, Senior Pastor,
Church of His Presence, Daphne, Alabama

Bob Sorge's life proclaims how to pursue and enjoy intimacy with God. His experience in the word, together with patient endurance, has given him living understanding on prayer. Gain fresh inspiration for the journey in which hang the very issues of life.

Mike Bickle, Director, Int'l House of Prayer,
Kansas City, Missouri

My dear friend Bob Sorge's passion for God and His word reverberates through every line. This wonderful book will fan the desperate flames of your love for Jesus.

Joy Dawson, Bible Teacher, Author

This book is more than just a good one-time read. It becomes your companion, living on your desk, traveling in your backpack. God's voice speaks from every page, revealing new insights with each read.

Karen Wheaton, The Ramp, Hamilton, Alabama

Contents

Part III: Setting A Marathon Pace

Part IV: Seeking A Deeper Relationship

About This Legacy Edition

Secrets of the Secret Place was first released in 2001 and is my most popular book. Twenty years later, it was time to polish it for posterity.

We're calling this the *Legacy Edition* and making it available in both paperback and hardcover. I labored to strengthen literally every sentence to make it more useful for coming generations, as the Lord tarries.

All the chapter titles remain the same, as does the general message of each chapter. While some material has been added, most of the changes are more nuanced—to make the book easier and more enjoyable to read.

The goal of this book is to strengthen and inspire the personal prayer life of every believer on earth. My prayer is that, as you're inspired to pray more consistently, your joy in walking with Christ will only grow.

Be strengthened in all the will of God!

Bob Sorge
Kansas City, Missouri
January, 2021

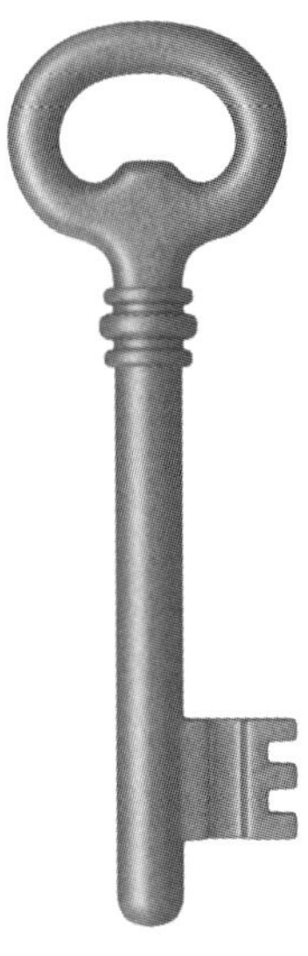

PART I

Accepting The Great Invitation

The great God of the universe has invited us to a breathing, growing relationship with Him—it's utterly astounding! In this first section, listen carefully and you'll hear His voice calling and compelling you to His secret place. Whether you choose to read a chapter a week, or take it at your own pace, may you have the wisdom to say yes to His incredible invitation.

CHAPTER ONE

The Secret of Saying "Yes"

Chris and DeeAnn Abke were feeling overwhelmed by a looming financial challenge. In desperation, they took some time late one evening—after settling their kids into bed—to seek the Lord's help. As they sat together on their living room couch, making their petitions known to God, suddenly an audible voice began to speak, "If you need help, call 9-1-1. If you need help, call 9-1-1."

They heard the voice say this about four or five times, and then it stopped. Mystified, Chris and DeeAnn just looked at each other.

The voice seemed to be coming from the garage, so they cautiously opened the door and flipped on the garage lights, not sure what they would find. Everything was in its place except for a small toy ambulance, belonging to their son, that lay by itself in the center of the garage floor.

Chris picked up the ambulance, pushed a button next to its emergency lights, and the voice began to speak, "If you need help, call 9-1-1." As they wondered aloud how the toy had activated of its own accord, suddenly the Holy Spirit seemed to nudge Chris with these words, "If you need help, call 9-1-1—Psalm 91:1." Going back to the Scriptures, the verse had an entirely new meaning to them as they read it together: "He who dwells in the secret place of the Most High shall abide under the shadow of the Almighty."

Chris and DeeAnn understood this as a divine invitation to renewed devotion in their secret place relationship with Him. If they would seek first the intimacy of abiding in the presence of the Almighty, the Lord would direct the supply of their financial needs.

I share my friends' story with you because I'm persuaded the power of heaven is unlocked when we devote ourselves to the secret place of the Most High. The purpose of this book, therefore, is to stoke the embers of your personal prayer life. May you say "Yes!" to a daily, fervent pursuit of Jesus in the secret place. *My prayer is that, with each chapter, you'll gain growing momentum to pursue the greatest pearl of human existence—a personal, passionate, vibrant relationship with your Creator.*

One of the best kept secrets of our faith is the blessedness of cultivating a secret life with God. Imagine the sheer delight of it even now. You're tucked away in a quiet nook; the door is shut; you're curled in a comfortable position; the living word of God is laid open before you; Jesus Himself is standing at your side; the Holy Spirit is gently washing your heart; as you meditate on His gracious words your love is awakened; your spirit is ignited; your mind is renewed; you talk to Him, and He talks to you; you speak the language of friendship.

Ahhh, it doesn't get any better than this!

But there are adversaries and hindrances. Hell will tempt, discourage, and lie to you about the delight and power of the secret place. The world will constantly try to distract and squeeze out your secret place time. Even the church sometimes depletes our energy for the secret place by getting us busy with other programs and activities.

Furthermore, few are the saints whose secret life in God is so compelling that it kindles others with a desire to follow their example.

Like many believers, I've been frustrated by the difference between what I *want* to do and what I *actually* do. On the one hand, I've had strong convictions about the importance of the secret place; on the other hand, I've struggled to maintain it as a consistent lifestyle. At times I've felt almost powerless to change my priorities concerning prayer.

We watch ourselves return persistently to the sources which are no source. For example, when wanting to be revitalized from a draining day, we'll turn on a film as though its distractions will renew us—only to be left empty for the umpteenth time. Or, we'll watch a YouTube sermon in the hope the preacher's walk will infuse us with fresh energy for the journey. But deep down we know that sermons and teachings, although edifying, can't replace the carrying power we find when we sit at His feet and hear His word for ourselves.

How do we find new momentum in the secret place? Not by beating up on ourselves, but by lifting our eyes to the hope set before us. My goal in this book is to share some secrets—lessons I've learned mostly by doing it wrong first—to empower you to reach for the upward call of God in Christ.

When we learn to dwell in the secret place of the Most High, we're positioned to discover the key to true kingdom fruitfulness. *Reproductive power is unlocked in the shadow of the Almighty.*

A great Bible example of this truth is found in the life of Cornelius, the first Gentile believer. Cornelius was a God-fearing Gentile who was devoted to prayer. His piety was described in the Book of Acts in four ways: he gave generously to the poor; he lived a holy lifestyle; he fasted; and he adhered to secret prayer. Because of those four pursuits, God filled Cornelius and his household with the Holy Spirit and made them the firstfruits of all Gentile believers.

It's as though God said, "Cornelius, your priority for secret prayer is an example I can reproduce in the nations. That's why I chose you to be the first Gentile to receive the Holy Spirit. I'm going to take your devotion to the secret place and export it to every nation on earth." What a powerful endorsement of Cornelius's hidden life with God. He became the catalyst for the redemption of the nations. I think he must stand in awe, in the great cloud of witnesses (Hebrews 12:1), at the way his faithful witness has shaken world history.

There's no telling the eruption of fruitfulness that can come from a life devoted to secret prayer in the shadow of the Most High.

You have a holy call to be a blessing to your family,

neighborhood, church, and city. As you devote yourself to your secret place, God will birth something in you that will spread, in His time, to the four corners of your sphere. It's a remarkable secret: *God's call burning in your breast will be uncontainable and unstoppable as you devote yourself to the fiery passion of intimate communion with the Lover of your soul.*

Won't you join me in pressing forward into new dimensions of kingdom power and glory? The face of Christianity is changed, generation to generation, by those who discover the power of the secret place. I pray that, with the reading of each page, you'll say *Yes* to the secret of the centuries.

What is that secret? someone might ask.

The secret place *is* the secret.

CHAPTER TWO

The Secret of the Shut Door

> But you, when you pray, go into your room, and when you have shut your door, pray to your Father who is in the secret place; and your Father who sees in secret will reward you openly (Matthew 6:6).

These words came from the Master's lips. All Scripture is God-breathed, but followers of Jesus always find particular delight in heeding the words Jesus Himself gave. When He taught on prayer, He gave primary emphasis to the secret place. In fact, His very first teaching on prayer (above) was on the primacy of the secret place. Later, He taught *how* to pray; but first, He told *where* to pray.

Matthew 6:6 contains a powerful secret regarding the *where* of prayer, but first let me ask a question. Do you occasionally feel disconnected from God? Do you sometimes struggle to feel God's presence when you pray? Do you wish you could know He's with you, right now, drawing near to you?

If your answer to any of those questions is *yes*, then I have some wonderful news for you. There's a guaranteed, surefire way to have instant intimacy with the Father any time you want, and Jesus Himself told the way. He gave us the key (above) when He said, *Your Father who is in the secret place.* Jesus was saying, *Your Father is already in the secret place. He has gone ahead of you and is waiting for you. The moment you get to the secret place, you're in the immediate presence of your Father.*

Jesus affirmed this truth twice in the same chapter. He said it a second time in Matthew 6:18, "So that you do not appear to men to be fasting, but to *your Father who is in the secret place*; and your Father who sees in secret will reward you openly." Jesus said it twice to emphasize with absolute certainty, *your Father is in the secret place.*

Furthermore, Jesus gave us the key to finding this secret place. To get there, all you have to do is *shut your door.*

When you enter a room and *shut your door*, you're in the presence of your Father. Instantly. Your shut door grants you instant intimacy with the Father. Even if you don't *feel* that intimacy right away, you can believe Jesus' assurance that it's true. You've just stepped into the Father's chamber. The secret place is your portal to the throne, the place where you taste of heaven itself. When you *know* you're with your Father, amazing changes will happen inside. You'll thrill with confidence in His nearness. As you reach for Him in faith, you'll actually begin to *feel* His presence. Your awareness of His presence will strengthen your faith and love.

Jesus painted a picture to help us visualize what's happening when we build our lives on a secret place relationship with God. We're getting our foundations in order. He said it's like building a house on rock:

> Therefore whoever hears these sayings of Mine, and does them, I will liken him to a wise man who built his house on the rock: and the rain descended, the floods came, and the winds blew and beat on that house; and it did not fall, for it was founded on the rock. But everyone who hears these sayings of Mine, and does not do them, will be like a foolish man who built his house on the sand: and the rain descended, the floods came, and the winds blew and beat on that house; and it fell. And great was its fall (Matthew 7:24-27).

Jesus was saying, *If you'll practice what I've just taught, you'll lay foundations in your life that will survive the harshest storms.* And storms will most certainly come. Storms come to all—to both the foolish and the wise. What distinguishes the wise from the foolish? Their foundation. When the storm comes, the wise remain standing.

Again, one of the most essential foundation stones for disciples is a secret life with God. Those who carefully nurture it will enjoy daily intimacy with the Father and will be prepared to sustain raging storms—whether they originate from hell's fury or the world's tribulations or the floodgates of heaven's blessings.

You have a guaranteed way to instant intimacy with the Father, every day. Don't forget the secret: *shut your door.*

CHAPTER THREE

The Secret of Listening

When God brought the people of Israel through the Red Sea to Mount Sinai, He came to them in a raging fire on the mountain and spoke with a thunderous voice. The encounter was completely overpowering.

The psalmist described this scene with an interesting phrase: *I answered you in the secret place of thunder* (Psalm 81:7). Mount Sinai was a *secret place* encounter between God and His people. In that desert, God spoke with them and give them His commandments.

The secret place is a place where God answers and speaks to us. Sometimes, He even thunders with His awesome voice. Nothing is more sustaining and life-giving than hearing His voice. God is always longing for an intimate relationship with His people in which we hear His voice and respond accordingly. We close the door to our secret place in order to shut out all distractions and tune our ears to the one voice we long to hear. *The secret place of thunder*—what an awesome description of the place where we come aside to be with our Lord!

Some people call their personal time with Jesus their *quiet time*, and that's not a wrong term to use, but what transpires here in the spirit realm is hardly quiet. *Thunderous* things rumble here that change the course of lives and generations.

On one occasion, the Lord showed me the most important word in the whole Bible. When I saw it, thunder resounded on my insides. Let me explain the context in which I received this insight.

I was in a season of consecration in which I was immersing myself in the words of Jesus. In other words, I was devouring the books of Matthew, Mark, Luke, and John, as well as the first three chapters of Revelation. While in that discipline, a certain word began to pop off the pages. *Hear.* Jesus used it over and over. "He who has ears to hear, let him hear!" (Matthew 13:9). How many times did He say it? Being alerted to this, I paid attention every time He spoke about hearing. The verses tumbled and hit me like a freight train. Suddenly, I saw it: *Hear* is the most important word in the Bible!

When the Lord showed me this, I wanted to underline every occurrence of *hear* in my Bible. The implications were profound. I realized that everything in the kingdom depends upon hearing His voice. When we hear, the greatest treasures of the kingdom open to us. This is the wellspring of eternal life; this is the fountainhead of kingdom power and authority; this is the source of wisdom, understanding, and counsel. Nothing can replace the confidence and authority that comes from hearing God. Things find their right alignment when we hear from God and act upon His word. Hearing God's voice has become the singular quest of my life. Nothing else can satisfy the deep longings of my heart.

Since everything in the kingdom is predicated upon hearing God, I advocate a prayer life comprised mostly of silent listening. Talking to God is delightful, but it's even more thrilling when He talks to us. I'm realizing He has more important things to say than I. *Things don't change when I talk to God; things change when God talks to me.* When I talk, nothing happens; when God talks, universes comes into existence. The power of prayer is not in convincing God of my agenda but in waiting on Him to receive His agenda.

Now, I don't mean to give the impression that I hear God's voice every day in prayer. I wish that were so! But most days I come away with unfulfilled longing, unanswered prayers, unrealized aspirations, deferred hope, and incomplete understanding. But then along comes one of those days—you probably know what I mean—when heaven leans over and God speaks something that's direct and personal. He breathes upon a Scripture and personalizes its meaning precisely to my felt needs. O what joy! That moment is worth all the knocking and seeking of the preceding days. I'll endure months of silence if He'll but speak one creative word from His mouth to my heart.

My role in the secret place is to listen for anything God might want to speak. He speaks, I listen. Even if He doesn't speak, time spent in listening isn't a waste but a relational investment. I hope to be found attentive when He's ready to speak. I can't tell God what or when to speak; but I can position myself in the secret place so that, when He does, I'm found listening.

Scripture says, "Today, if you will hear His voice" (Psalm 95:7). Hearing His voice, then, involves our will. We must *choose* to hear Him. How? By deciding to set aside the time to listen. And we do it *today*, because hearing is a *today* thing. The verse says "if" because hearing His voice is conditional upon our engaging with Him. Will we take the time to stop and listen?

All of us want God to hear our prayers. But the Lord said, "Therefore it happened, that just as He proclaimed and they would not hear, so they called out and I would not listen" (Zechariah 7:13). In other words, God was saying, *When I spoke, you didn't listen to Me; therefore, when you speak, I won't listen to you.* The inference is that if we'll listen for His voice, He'll listen for ours.

Oh, how can I speak of this wondrous secret more articulately? How can I make it more plain? Hearing God is the most cherished secret of the secret place.

Don't believe the adversary's lies. He wants you to think you're unable to hear God's voice. It's just not true. Jesus had you in mind when He said, "My sheep hear My voice, and I know them, and they follow Me" (John 10:27). You *are* His sheep and you *can* hear His voice. Stop everything, come aside, listen, and wait on Him. Wait until. He longs to visit with you.

When trying to listen, many of us get bombarded with thoughts about various duties that need to be done. So, here's a practical suggestion: Take a notepad to the secret place and write down *Things To Do* as they pop into your head. With them written down, you know you won't forget them later. Now you can relax and return your focus to listening.

If you find quiet listening a challenging discipline to master, you're certainly not alone. It's rigorous, and most of us aren't exercised in it. But be encouraged—the rigor of the exercise points to the vigor of the reward. One moment with God can be worth a lifetime of waiting. Resolve to make attentive listening a lifelong pursuit. It'll become easier in the doing, and you'll master your own delightful cadence with God.

Just one word from God and doors open, decisions land, fears vanish, and seasons change. *Hear Him!*

CHAPTER FOUR

The Secret of Radical Obedience

Hearing God through the word is one of the greatest secrets of the overcoming life. However, it must be followed by its corollary: radical obedience. We hear, and then we act. "But be doers of the word, and not hearers only, deceiving yourselves" (James 1:22).

By *radical obedience* I mean immediate action that fulfills the commandment to its fullest measure. *Radical obedience does not seek to comply to the minimal standards but pursues extravagant, lavish fulfillment.* If Jesus says, *Sell all*, then we sell all. Immediately.

The New Testament Greek word for obedience (*hupakoe*) is a compound of two words, under (*hupo)* and hear (*akouo).* Obedience means *to hear under*. We *hear* with a heart that comes *under* the authority of the word spoken. When God speaks, we submit to His authority and obey.

Obedience starts not with activity but with sitting and hearing. Devotion to the secret place is the saint's first great act of obedience. Jesus revealed this:

> But He answered them, saying, "Who is My mother, or My brothers?" And He looked around in a circle at those who sat about Him, and said, "Here are My mother and My brothers! For whoever does the will of God is My brother and My sister and mother" (Mark 3:33-35).

The will of God in that moment was for the people to sit at Jesus' feet and hear His word. Sitting and listening for His word is still our first duty. We do this primarily by devoting ourselves to the secret place. Once we receive His word we can devote ourselves to radical obedience. It's a matter of priorities. *First we sit and listen, and then we go and do.*

My friend, Steve Peglow, once told me he thought some people were *common law Christians.* By that he meant they want the benefits of living with Jesus without making the commitment. A couple will find the full joy of living together only when they covenant to each other in marriage; in the same way, the joy of following Jesus is found only in promising to fulfill every word that comes from His mouth.

Some folks put their best energies into creative thinking. But sometimes God frustrates the plans of people: "The Lord brings the counsel of the nations to nothing; He makes the plans of the peoples of no effect. The counsel of the Lord stands forever" (Psalm 33:10-11). Focus your best energy, therefore, not on being creative but obedient. Devote your most alert moments to prayer. Wait in His presence, listen for His voice, and then follow His word. Why labor to generate your own ideas when it's only God's counsel that will stand? I'm saying it several different ways: The key is in hearing and obeying.

Here are just four of the many benefits of obedience:

Obedience unlocks eternal life

Jesus said, "I know that His command is everlasting life" (John 12:50). Coming from the Master of understatement, these simple words contain wider implications than a cursory reading reveals. Take that statement to your secret place and meditate on it. Let Him awaken you to the life-giving power that flows from adherence to His word. *The life coursing through Him flows into you when you obey.*

Obedience obtains the gaze of God

God looks with special interest and affection upon those devoted to obedience. He said it this way, "But on this one will I look: on him who is poor and of a contrite spirit, and *who trembles at My word*" (Isaiah 66:2). Just imagine it: You're in the secret place with His word before you, and you're trembling at the prospect of His speaking to you; He sees your willing spirit and conceives of ways to honor your devotion. Wow! To tremble at His word means at least four things: We long to hear it, we're eager to understand it, we bow before its authority, and we're diligent to act on it. *When we tremble for His word with this kind of keen anticipation, He draws close and looks on us with favor.*

Obedience produces greater intimacy

In my opinion, one of the most powerful statements Jesus made is right here: "He who has My commandments and keeps them, it is he who loves Me. And he who loves Me will be loved by My Father, and I will love him and manifest Myself to him" (John 14:21). Jesus said obedience is the proof of love, and love brings us into incredible intimacy with the Father. Furthermore, obedience unlocks the affections of Christ and His self-disclosure to the human heart. We long for nothing more than for Jesus to manifest Himself to us! Because of that longing, we embrace any and every command of His mouth. We delight in obedience because His presence is so sweet when we keep His commands. Obedience is a doorway to zeal, fire, closeness, knowing, and being known.

Obedience lays unshakable foundations

> "Therefore whoever hears these sayings of Mine, and does them, I will liken him to a wise man who built his house on the rock: and the rain descended, the floods came, and the winds blew and beat on that house; and it did not fall, for it was founded on the rock. But everyone who hears these sayings of Mine, and does not do them, will be like a foolish man who built his house on the sand: and the rain descended, the floods came, and the winds blew and beat on that house; and it fell. And great was its fall" (Matthew 7:24-27).

Jesus acknowledged that storms come both to those who do His sayings and those who don't. No one is exempt. The question is not whether storms will come your way, but whether you'll survive. Will your foundations be strong enough to sustain the coming winds and floods? Those who walk in radical obedience will weather the storm and overcome. In fact, the storm will actually accentuate their righteousness, as Isaiah testified: "Oh, that you had heeded My commandments! Then your peace would have been like a river, and *your righteousness like the waves of the sea*" (Isaiah 48:18). When stormy winds assail the righteous. their righteousness rises like mighty breakers, crashing on the shore in majestic thunderings of fragrance to God.

Of course, there are other benefits of obedience beyond these four just cited. But I'm trying to keep these chapters short! Consider just two other brief thoughts regarding obedience. The first comes to us through Mary, the mother of Jesus.

At the wedding in Cana, Mary said to the servants, "Whatever He says to you, do it" (John 2:5). That summarizes the essence of obedience. We hear what He says and we do it. Servants don't try to give the Master a better idea; servants don't complain that they think the task is stupid; servants don't pause to consider whether they're in the mood to do it; servants don't decide if the task is within their dignity to perform. They just do it. "So likewise you, when you have done all those things which you are commanded, say, 'We are unprofitable servants. We have done what was our duty to do'" (Luke 17:10).

The closer you get to God, the more obedient you must be. I see this principle in the life of Moses. The people of Israel saw God's acts and sought to obey Him by avoiding sin and choosing righteousness. But that elementary level of obedience wasn't sufficient for Moses. Moses knew God's ways (Psalm 103:7), and his nearness to God necessitated a higher level of obedience. The issue for Moses was no longer simply, *Is this action right or wrong?* The issue was, *What is God's command?* For example, when Moses was on the fiery mountain the command was basically, *Stay behind the cleft of the rock. If you come out from behind the protective rock and see My face, you'll die. You're so close to Me right now, Moses, that if you make a wrong move and see My face, you'll have a cardiac arrest on the spot.* (See Exodus 33:20-23.) Now, is there anything inherently sinful about stepping out from behind a wall of rock? No. But when you're that close to God, implicit obedience becomes more imperative than ever.

Be like Moses. Get close to God in the secret place, and then obey every word. Because the closer you get to God, the more obedient you must be.

CHAPTER FIVE

The Secret of Rapid Repentance

Eight times the Scriptures charge us, *Take heed to yourselves.* Two of those times the words are spoken by Jesus Himself. Taking heed to ourselves is a primary focus of the secret place. *Prayer is the constant calibration of the soul.* We stop to take careful spiritual inventory. We're not paranoid around God, as though we're uncertain of our status with Him. Rather, we're wise to check and make sure that nothing is hindering our race or growth. We self-test, therefore, for spiritual fervor, alertness, faithfulness, purity, love, obedience, growth in grace, etc.

In the secret place, *my spirit makes diligent search* (Psalm 77:6). It reaches and searches to perceive what God is thinking about everything in my life. Because I long to please Him and know His will more deeply, I search to identify if there's anything He wants me to change. I want to be sure I'm holding nothing that could hinder our relationship.

When I'm in the word, if He shows me anything I need to deal with, then I'm eager to respond immediately. I call it *rapid repentance.* It's immediate, thorough, wholehearted repentance. If He shows it to me, I'm getting rid of it. Fast.

Want some good advice? *Become a good repenter.* It's how we keep moving forward with God. If pride tries to hinder you from repenting, kill the thing. You're a wretch. You need mercy so badly it's scary. Wise up and master the art of repentance. Call your sin in its worst possible terms. Abhor yourself (Job 42:6). Grovel. Eat dust.

Learn a secret from David. One reason he found such favor with God, in spite of all his miserable failures, was because he was such a thorough repenter. God loved that about David!

Personally, I've always tended to feel a little self-congratulatory about my heart and intentions. I mean, can't God see what a good, sincere heart I have? But then the Lord used the story of the multiplying of loaves and fish to help me see how far below His glory I actually live.

In that story, when the disciples saw a hungry multitude of people, Jesus asked Philip, "Where shall we buy bread, that these may eat?" (John 6:5). But Jesus was testing Philip with this question because He already knew how He was going to multiply the food for everyone. The test for Philip was, *are you living in the glory realm where Jesus lives?* If he was, his answer would be something like, *Lord, just break open these loaves and fish and multiply them for the multitude.* But that wasn't his answer. Philip failed the test because his thoughts were a universe below those of Jesus (Isaiah 55:9).

Then I saw it: I'm failing the Philip test *all the time!* I'm so earthbound in my orientation that I'm almost oblivious to the dimension of glory in which Jesus lives. It's safe to assume that, apart from God's grace, I'm constantly falling short of the excellence of God's glory. Do I need to repent continually? You bet!

Beloved, I pray you might gain the secret of radical, rapid repentance. Ready repentance opens the channels for intimate communion with Jesus. When you're in the secret place, be quick to confess your unbelief and hardness of heart. Don't make Him talk you into it. Agree quickly with Him in the way (Matthew 5:25).

When I speak of repentance, I'm not thinking only of repenting from sins like lying, fornication, stealing, cursing, pornography, hatred, drunkenness, anger, or not tithing. Those sins are so obvious that you hardly even need the conviction of the Holy Spirit to know you're in disobedience. God's word on such matters is crystal clear. Repenting of these kinds of outward sins is Christianity 101.

No, I'm thinking of going beyond the *obvious* to what

Scripture calls *iniquities*. Iniquities are hidden faults we often don't even realize we have. We have wicked iniquities because our fallen nature has discolored the fabric of our thoughts, motives, feelings, responses, and desires. We all sin in a host of *subtle* ways—such as pride, rebellion, unbelief, envy, selfishness, ambition, and covetousness.

Again, most of us don't even see the hidden iniquities of our hearts. God knows we can't repent of something we don't see, so He helps by showing us our iniquities—little by little. We don't go looking for them in our own understanding, but when He reveals them to us, we repent immediately and completely. No need to obsess on introspection, but just respond quickly when the Holy Spirit reveals the iniquity of your heart.

Repenting of iniquity is fundamental to the kingdom:

> Nevertheless the solid foundation of God stands, having this seal: "The Lord knows those who are His," and, "Let everyone who names the name of Christ depart from iniquity." But in a great house there are not only vessels of gold and silver, but also of wood and clay, some for honor and some for dishonor. Therefore if anyone cleanses himself from the latter, he will be a vessel for honor, sanctified and useful for the Master, prepared for every good work (2 Timothy 2:19-21).

Paul was saying the Christian life is founded on two powerful realities: We are known by Christ, and we depart from iniquity when we see it.

As you meditate in the word in the secret place, God uses the fire of circumstances and the fire of His word to reveal your hidden faults to you. Like Job and Isaiah, when we see God in a new way, we can't help but see how vile we are, and we're empowered to repent (Job 42:5-6; Isaiah 6:1-5). When you see God, you'll be overwhelmed at how much He accepts you unconditionally, and also how unrelentingly committed He is to your changing. When your issues are revealed in the light of His glory, it's time for rapid repentance!

For the devout, repentance isn't morbid but full of hope and promise. It's an opportunity to turn from things that have been hindering love. When the Holy Spirit reveals the iniquity of our heart and we respond eagerly in repentance, we experience the rush of the Father's pleasure. His countenance warms our hearts and we actually *feel* the nearness of His delight.

When we repent of our iniquities, Jesus called this *buying gold in the fire* (Revelation 3:18). It's through rapid, regular repentance that we buy the gold of Christ-like character. Proven vessels of gold and silver are useful to the Master for noble purposes (2 Timothy 2:21). Those who resist repentance limit their usefulness to the Master. Vessels of wood or clay are useful to the Master for less honorable purposes. In a great house there's a need even for toilet plungers.

Here's the bottom line. When He shows the iniquity of your heart, repent eagerly and immediately. David would tell you, it's the secret to getting on with God.

CHAPTER SIX

The Secret of Sowing

> Do not be deceived, God is not mocked; for whatever a man sows, that he will also reap. For he who sows to his flesh will of the flesh reap corruption, but he who sows to the Spirit will of the Spirit reap everlasting life. And let us not grow weary while doing good, for in due season we shall reap if we do not lose heart (Galatians 6:7-9).

One of our most common struggles, when it comes to the secret place, is to feel like we're "spinning our wheels"—that our time invested in prayer and contemplation is accomplishing little. When we feel that way, it's tempting to lose heart and just move on to something else with a shrug that says, *Well, maybe it will be better next time.*

Some of us have become so discouraged with feelings of ineffectiveness that we've fallen into a slump of neglect. I hope the message of this chapter will help get you back on track.

Here's the marvelous secret of Galatians 6: *If you'll sow to the Spirit, you'll eventually reap to the Spirit.* Eventually. Said another way, if you'll sow to the word you'll eventually reap to the word. If you'll sow to the secret place, you'll eventually reap to the secret place.

It's impossible to keep sowing to the secret place—every day at the feet of Jesus, every day taking in His word—without eventually reaping spiritual *life*. We've often applied this text to the grace of financial giving, but it applies equally to the grace of investing in prayer. If you'll keep sowing in the word and prayer, you'll eventually reap in a way that will put a new glint in your eyes and a fresh spring in your step.

When we speak of sowing, we mean devoting *time* to the secret place—even when it doesn't feel productive in the moment. Why? Because we believe in the law of reaping. There's always a delay between sowing and reaping. We sow today for a harvest tomorrow. What kind of harvest will we reap? A relational walk with Jesus that is truly living and vibrant. The change in us will, in turn, impact everything around us.

This secret has carried me in times when I've been tempted to relax the intensity of my pursuit. For example, when I've been on fasting retreats, I've sometimes been tempted to abort the fast because it seems to be accomplishing nothing. Just when I'm tempted to quit, I remind myself that if I'll continue to sow, one day I'll reap. I lift my focus from my current frustrations and renew my confidence in God's promise that a harvest always comes, in time, to those who persevere.

Have I ever experienced such a harvest? Yes! After persevering in sowing, I've had moments in the secret place when the Holy Spirit has suddenly given me an infusion of divine life. It almost always comes through the word. He speaks a word that flushes my cheeks and enables me to keep walking in my wilderness.

Some words I've received have been *sleepers*. What I mean is, in the moment the insight didn't seem that significant; but in the days following, my appreciation for that insight grew until I realized I had been hit with true spiritual life. My resolve to sow *now* ended up producing a strong spiritual harvest *later*.

We live in an age that wants to see immediate results. Life can become a race to produce—which can rob us of investing in the secret place. But spiritual growth can't be measured by lists of accomplished tasks and met deadlines. Our devotional life is more like the planting of a garden. After sowing to the secret place, we usually can't point to immediate results or benefits. The results of what we sow today may not manifest until the season comes to maturation.

Sowing is often mundane, boring, and laborious. Rarely are the benefits of sowing seen immediately. Wise believers who understand this will devote themselves consistently to arduous sowing, knowing they'll eventually reap if they don't lose heart. This is the principle of Proverbs 12:11, "He who tills his land will be satisfied with bread." No tilling, no bread. To enjoy a harvest, we must till—make room in—the soil of our hearts for the implanted word. Once planted in a good heart, God's word is so powerful that nothing can stop its eventual harvest.

Every moment you spend in the secret place is an investment in your eternal inheritance. God sees the devotion of your labor and strategizes how to honor it. The seeds you sow now will produce a harvest you'll enjoy *forever*.

So whatever you do, *don't quit!* When you feel ineffectual, knuckle down, get stubborn, and invest even more. The word being sown in your heart today is going to germinate, sprout, push roots downward, thrust branches upward, and produce fruit. *Catch the secret: Those who sow will most assuredly reap!*

CHAPTER SEVEN

The Secret of Refuge

There *is* a refuge from the storms of life. While some storms can't be avoided, there *is* a place to hide. That place, of course, is the secret place. David wrote about it.

> For in the time of trouble He shall hide me in His pavilion; in the secret place of His tabernacle He shall hide me; He shall set me high upon a rock (Psalm 27:5).
>
> You shall hide them in the secret place of Your presence from the plots of man; You shall keep them secretly in a pavilion from the strife of tongues (Psalm 31:20).

In speaking of *the secret place* in these verses, David had in view the sanctuary or pavilion of God's presence where He hides His beloved. Webster's dictionary defines sanctuary as *a place of refuge; asylum; hence, immunity*. God's embrace is a sanctuary for the war-weary soldier, a place of immunity from the enemy's attacks.

Here you can find shelter from the swirl of emotions that assault your soul. Here you can vent your anxious thoughts. Here you can be renewed in love. Here you can gaze on the Lord's beauty. You'll hear your Father's promises of protection; you'll be healed from the wounds of man's rejection; you'll regain strength for the journey; you'll be safe; you'll live again.

The secret place is like the eye of a hurricane. While all is storming around us, we're locked in an inner sanctuary of rest and peace. Sometimes it feels paradoxical because we're in a place of both storm and peace simultaneously. When we retreat to the secret place, the storm doesn't stop; in fact, sometimes it actually seems to *escalate* in intensity.

When you intensify your pursuit of God, sometimes the storms get even worse. Satan won't let you take new territory without a fight. Francis Frangipane described it with the phrase, "New levels, new devils." Some get offended by this because they expected God to honor their renewed fervor with tranquility and serenity. They had a promise of refuge but suddenly found themselves in even greater turbulence and warfare. Why might this happen? The answer is paradoxical.

While the place of prayer is a place of immunity, it's also a place of increased satanic attack. Let me mention some biblical examples. When seeking to destroy Daniel, the only chink in his armor that his enemies could find was his prayer life. They watched for him to pray to the God of heaven and then they pounced. Where did Satan tempt Jesus? During His forty-day fast in the wilderness. Where did Judas betray Jesus to His tormentors? In Jesus' prayer garden—Gethsemane.

Sometimes we experience similar assaults. Your secret place can be both a sanctuary and a war zone. When you're attacked in the place of prayer, however, be assured of this: your Father is exercising sovereign jurisdiction over the entire affair. *Nothing can happen to you in the secret place that He doesn't specifically allow and design for His higher purposes.* You're totally immune from anything outside His will.

Psalm 91 deals with this tension of safety versus turbulence. The psalm launches with this powerful assurance, "He who dwells in the secret place of the Most High shall abide under the shadow of the Almighty." And we think, *Great! Nothing can touch me here!* But the remainder of the psalm seems to contradict that notion. Verse 3 speaks of being snared by the fowler and being caught by perilous pestilence. Yes, God delivers us from those things; but initially we're distressed by their grip. The psalm also describes terrors of the night, arrows that fly by day, pestilence that walks in darkness, and destruction that lays waste at noonday. Being under the shadow of the Almighty doesn't mean we're exempt from storms; but it does mean He's with us in the storm and He'll bring us through to deliverance.

Psalm 91 also promises uncommon refuge for those who learn to abide in Christ: "A thousand may fall at your side, and ten thousand at your right hand; but it shall not come near you" (Psalm 91:7). Even if your fellow comrades are falling around you by the thousands, you will experience uncommon preservation. He preserves you because you have made Him your refuge.

May you have grace to make a heroic decision: Lose your life and pursue the secret place of the Most High. It's the way of the cross. The cross is where we sustain unprecedented assaults and unparalleled intimacy. There's no safer place in the universe than His bosom.

O how I long to direct your heart to this place of refuge! Are winds swirling about your head? Run into the Lord! A refuge is something you *flee into*. A refuge doesn't automatically erect itself around you; to find safe harbor, you must seek it out and run into its shelter. As the Scriptures say, "That by two immutable things, in which it is impossible for God to lie, we might have strong consolation, *who have fled for refuge* to lay hold of the hope set before us" (Hebrews 6:18). If God is to be your refuge, you must flee to Him. The cry is, "Oh Lord, I am about to be consumed—I run into You! Hide me!"

"Be my strong refuge, to which I may resort continually" (Psalm 71:3). *Resort continually*. Therein lies the secret.

CHAPTER EIGHT

The Secret of Decision Making

Are you facing an important decision and not sure what to do? *Run into the secret place.* Because it's important to God not only *what* but also *how* you decide. For example, it's possible to make the right choice but yet be distant from Him. He wants us making decisions from the wellspring of nearness.

When facing major decisions, Jesus showed us how by going to the secret place. For example, when it was time to appoint the twelve apostles, those choices were so important—historic in implications—that He got alone with His Father in prayer.

> Now it came to pass in those days that He went out to the mountain to pray, and continued all night in prayer to God. And when it was day, He called His disciples to Himself; and from them He chose twelve whom He also named apostles: Simon, whom He also named Peter, and Andrew his brother; James and John; Philip and Bartholomew; Matthew and Thomas; James the son of Alphaeus, and Simon called the Zealot; Judas the son of James, and Judas Iscariot who also became a traitor (Luke 6:12-16).

Even the choice of Judas, His betrayer, was bathed in prayer. In fact, the selection of Judas was *especially* bathed in prayer because He knew that choice would culminate in his horrific destruction. Such a weighty decision necessitated a nightlong session of solitary prayer.

Disciples of Jesus make important decisions from that same place of intimate prayer.

Your loving heavenly Father is deeply invested in all your affairs and He wants to help in all your decision making. He said so here:

> I will instruct you and teach you in the way you should go; I will guide you with My eye. Do not be like the horse or like the mule, which have no understanding, which must be harnessed with bit and bridle, else they will not come near you (Psalm 32:8-9).

Notice the final phrase, "Else they will not come near you." The horse and mule must be harnessed with bit and bridle if you're to get them close. They won't draw near volitionally.

The passage describes divine guidance received from a place of relational closeness. The Lord was saying, *I don't want to yank and jerk you around in order to get you on course. I want you to draw close—real close—so I can direct your steps in the context of an enjoyable relationship.*

The Lord said the horse and mule *have no understanding*, and that's why they don't come near. They don't understand, for starters, that proximity to the Master is *wisdom*. An unharnessed horse is likely to charge ahead of its master; an unharnessed mule is likely to drag behind. Either mode makes their energies counter-productive to the master.

Some people are mulish. They just don't get it. They pull away foolishly from their source of life and care. It hasn't penetrated their thick skulls that the smartest place in the universe is right next to Him. The wisest thing you'll ever do is draw close to God and lean on Him with all your heart.

As you pursue this proximity, you'll begin to unlock the greatest secrets of life. Here He guides with an eye that sees everything from beginning to end. Sometimes we make life choices based on our analysis of all the pros and cons, but there's a better way. Instead of looking *outward,* we're invited to look *upward*. What an adventure—to receive life direction by beholding His beauty, enjoying His company, and receiving the guidance of His gaze. Consider the vantage His throne gives Him. His eyes miss nothing! Gaze on His mouth until He speaks to you. Look into His eye until He shows you the way to walk.

Those who make decisions based on observable data become *thermometers* of society; but those who decide based on what they see in God become *thermostats* of society. They shape their world by bringing heavenly initiatives to earthly spheres.

Intimacy precedes insight. Passion precedes purpose. First comes the secret place, then comes divine guidance. God doesn't simply want to get you on the right path, He wants to enjoy you in the journey. When some folks know His will, they're finished with prayer and take off running. But He wants to keep the conversation going during the mission. He wants to know you and be known.

Again, pursuing an intimate relationship with God in the secret place is the smartest thing you'll do. You'll discover your destiny in life and you'll come to know Him. So stop right here. No need to read the next chapter just yet. Set this book down and find a quiet corner with your Friend. Talk to Him about the options in front of you. He wants you to make this decision *together*. Get close and catch His eye!

CHAPTER NINE

The Secret of No Plan B

One of the sweetest secrets to intimacy with Jesus is to come to Him as your only source of help and hope. *Lord, in this situation I have no Plan B—no other option or backup plan. I look to You alone. Help me, for You are my only help.* He *loves* it when we look to Him alone for deliverance. And conversely, His jealousy is stirred when we entertain other saviors.

The Israelites were frequently tempted to turn to false gods for help. In response, the Lord scoffed at their idolatry by pointing to the vain hope that a block of wood offered:

> He cuts down cedars for himself, and takes the cypress and the oak; he secures it for himself among the trees of the forest. He plants a pine, and the rain nourishes it. Then it shall be for a man to burn, for he will take some of it and warm himself; yes, he kindles it and bakes bread; indeed he makes a god and worships it; he makes it a carved image, and falls down to it. He burns half of it in the fire; with this half he eats meat; he roasts a roast, and is satisfied. He even warms himself and says, "Ah! I am warm, I have seen the fire." And the rest of it he makes into a god, his carved image. He falls down before it and worships it, prays to it and says, "Deliver me, for you are my god!" They do not know nor understand; for He has shut their eyes, so that they cannot see, and their hearts, so that they cannot understand. And no one considers in his heart, nor is there knowledge nor understanding to say, "I have burned half of it in the fire, yes, I have also baked bread on its coals; I have roasted meat and eaten it; and shall I make the rest of it an abomination? Shall I fall down before a block of wood?" He feeds on ashes; a deceived heart has turned him aside; and he cannot deliver his soul, nor say, "Is there not a lie in my right hand?" (Isaiah 44:14-20).

The Lord quoted idolaters as saying to a block of wood, "Deliver me, for you are my god!" We can conclude, then, that a false god is *anything to which we ascribe the power of deliverance*. This definition helps me see that, even though very few today worship figurines of wood or stone, we still have many false gods—sources we think can deliver us.

What are some of the things to which we sometimes turn because we see in them the power of deliverance? (let the reader understand):

- Money
- Health insurance
- Medical treatment, prescriptions
- Social Security
- Retirement plans, IRA's
- Credit cards, loans
- Drugs, alcohol
- Pleasure, entertainment, recreation, sports
- Sex
- Social circles, friends
- Counselors
- Lawsuits
- Declaring bankruptcy
- etc.

Saviors such as these campaign for our allegiance. At every turn, the gods of our age commend their powers. Television commercials promote all kinds of relief: *Try me! Let me heal your pain. I am your answer. Look no further. Buy me and I will deliver you.*

Something dynamic happens within when you look at some of those sources of deliverance and say, *No! God, You alone are my Deliverer!* This kind of singular affection can move the Father to respond in ways that wow the heart and tenderize the spirit. The realms of intimacy here are quite without parallel.

Depending on God alone can be a risky, wild ride. For

example, the Israelites risked everything when they walked down into the Red Sea, even though the land was dry. It was also a wild ride because, when the Egyptians attempted to do so, they drowned (Hebrews 11:29). People of faith do things that, if attempted by others, would be fatal.

True worshipers are those who come to God *first* in time of need. They seek His face and wait to receive directions for the next step. The secret place is the threshold where they pause, seek His intervention, and cry for wisdom and revelation.

Occasionally, the Spirit will say things like, *In this situation, I want you to wait on Me and stand in faith until I sovereignly intervene.* When God gives you this word, *fasten your seatbelt.* You're probably in for the ride of your life. You're stepping into the God zone. Here we find the stuff of miracles. This is where God rises up in vengeance and wreaks havoc upon our enemies. Our role is to gaze on Him, love Him, and grow in enduring faith; His role is to loose resurrection power in His time and way. Not every crisis you face falls into this category but, when it does, tighten your belt. You're following the high road of the greatest saints of history—where you'll see the power of His arm, the splendor of His beauty, and the mysteries of His purpose.

David sang about this high road:

> My soul, wait silently for God alone, for my expectation is from Him. He only is my rock and my salvation; He is my defense; I shall not be moved. In God is my salvation and my glory; the rock of my strength, and my refuge, is in God. Trust in Him at all times, you people; pour out your heart before Him; God is a refuge for us. Selah (Psalm 62:5-8).

David's call to wait on God alone resonates for me personally because, as of this writing, I suffer from a longtime physical infirmity. To wait on God alone means, at least for me, to wait on Him for His promised healing. Through the years, I've been tempted to consider other avenues of relief, especially as the skillfulness of medical procedures have advanced. But in regard to this infirmity, I've chosen to hold to His promise and say, *You alone are my Helper. If You don't save me, I'm not saved. If You don't heal me, I'm not healed. If You don't deliver me, I'm not delivered. If I can't get it in You, I'll go without. I have no other recourse, no Plan B, no alternative. It's You and You alone. I worship You. You are my God!*

This is the *single eye* to which Jesus pointed when He said, "If therefore your eye is good, your whole body will be full of light" (Matthew 6:22). The King James Version reads, *If therefore thine eye be single*. Whether translated *good* or *single*, the original Greek word means to be void of duplicity, having singular focus. When your eye is focused on God alone as your Savior and Deliverer, you open to the fullness of light He destines to fill your entire being.

David prayed for singular focus: "Unite my heart to fear Your name" (Psalm 86:11). He was basically asking, "Lord, give me an undivided heart, a single focus that sees only You as the sovereign power to be feared and worshiped."

I've learned that the Lord will test us to prove our ownership of this reality. He'll allow storms to see if we'll reach reflexively for any source of relief within our grasp. Will we exhaust all our options and then turn to Him finally, almost as a last resort?

Perhaps we need to change how we view the storms of life. Can we see God using our storms strategically to guide us to higher kingdom living? Can we approach life's trials as divine invitations to elevate to His realm of faith?

There's a great secret here to be learned: When the storm hits, run into the secret place. Establish your spirit in grace and say to Him with a steadfast heart, *You alone are my expectation*. Our Savior watches to prove Himself strong on behalf of those who have no other gods before Him.

CHAPTER TEN

The Secret of Burning

It's the secret place that lights our fire and sets us burning. It fuels a white-hot, fiery zeal for the face of Jesus and the concerns of His kingdom. Jesus came to kindle a fire on earth (Luke 12:49) so we might be set ablaze with His passions and desires. To maintain the flame, we must stoke it constantly in the inner alcove of the secret place.

You're destined for fire. You're going to burn for eternity—the only question is *where*. But you've made your choice. You've decided to be a living flame, ignited with the exhilaration of beholding His beauty, worshiping Him with uninhibited abandon, and deployed to the world with calculated zeal. You don't love your life even unto death. You have something to live for because you have something to die for. You refuse to wallow in middle-American Christianity. You won't settle for anything less than being a firebrand of holiness.

God's word is a fire (Jeremiah 23:29), and His presence is totally engulfed in fire (Ezekiel 1:4, 27; Daniel 7:9). When you approach Him, you're drawing near the greatest inferno of the universe. *To catch His fire, get close.* When you feel distant and disengaged spiritually, retreat to the closet, place your cold heart before the fireplace of His word, and allow His truth and Spirit to restore your fervency. Don't despair over your dullness. Your resistant soul is no match for the fire of His heart! Get close, draw near to His fiery love, and let Him who is Jealous kindle you with His love (Exodus 24:14).

The secret to staying fervent for Jesus is not in responding to altar calls (as good as those are); it's not in having someone lay hands on you and pray for you (as valid as that is); it's not in listening to a good sermon or a passionate worship playlist; love stays white-hot by devoting yourself consistently to the place-of-the-shut-door. Behind the lattice, as you gaze unveiled on His glory (2 Corinthians 3:18), the *spirit of burning* (Isaiah 4:4) will ignite your soul.

Do you want a stronger motivation for the secret place? Invite the Burning One—the Holy Spirit—to ignite His fiery jealousy in your heart. The Scripture says, "The Spirit who dwells in us yearns jealously" (James 4:5). The aim of His jealous yearning is that we might burn with fiery passion for our Beloved and for Him alone. You may want to whisper this sublime prayer right now, "Holy Spirit, let Your burning jealousy engulf me until every competing affection is reduced to ashes and all that's left is a raging, all-consuming passion—love for the altogether Lovely One, the Man Christ Jesus!"

When John saw the Holy Spirit at the throne of God, he described His fire in this glorious manner: "Seven lamps of fire were burning before the throne, which are the seven Spirits of God" (Revelation 4:5). The Holy Spirit is *burning before the throne.* That describes perfectly what I want to do. I won't relent until I, too, am *burning before the throne.*

As one who longs to burn for God, I've looked at Proverbs 6:27-28 differently from its immediate meaning. Those verses portray the harmful effects of adultery, but in a metaphorical way, they could also be said to describe our secret place with God:

> Can a man take fire to his bosom, and his clothes not be burned? Can one walk on hot coals, and his feet not be seared? (Proverbs 6:27-28).

When you take time to contemplate God's word, you're actually taking fire into your bosom—because *His word is a fire* (Jeremiah 23:29). His word is able to incinerate the filthy, leprous clothes of your old life. And as you stand and burn before the throne, you're walking *back and forth in the midst of fiery stones* (Ezekiel 28:14). The hot coals of His holy mountain will sear your feet to walk in holiness, righteousness, and obedience.

"Can a man take fire to his bosom, and his clothes not be burned?" (Proverbs 6:27) The answer is, *No!* Clutch His fire to your bosom and everything about your life will be different. It's impossible to embrace these embers and remain unchanged. *O Lord, we draw Your fire to our bosom with trembling anticipation.*

John the Baptist was a man who burned for God. God took him aside to the solitude of the wilderness in order to set him on fire. When he was finally released to his generation, he was a living flame. Notice that in the following verses thrice Jesus asked, *What did you go out to see?*

> As they departed, Jesus began to say to the multitudes concerning John: "*What did you go out into the wilderness to see?* A reed shaken by the wind? *But what did you go out to see?* A man clothed in soft garments? Indeed, those who wear soft clothing are in kings' houses. *But what did you go out to see?* A prophet? Yes, I say to you, and more than a prophet" (Matthew 11:7-9).

Jesus testified that the people didn't go to the wilderness primarily to *hear* something, but to *see* something. They made the trip so they could watch a man whom Jesus called *the burning and shining lamp* (John 5:35). In the secret place of the wilderness, John the Baptist's love was incubated and kindled. Set on fire from heaven, He became a shining lamp for the entire nation. The people came from all over to see the flame and be enlightened by the lamp. Because everybody likes a bonfire.

Do something dangerous—get alone with God! Set your love on Him, minister to Him, and burn before the throne. His fire will consume all but love itself. Here's the secret: *He makes His ministers a flame of fire* (Hebrews 1:7). Stand and minister to Him and He'll make *you* a flame of fire, too.

CHAPTER 11

The Secret of Violence

The term *spiritual violence* captures the intensity with which the last days' generation will pursue God. Denying themselves, they'll lay aside all entangling sins. They'll run their race wholeheartedly with passion, purity, and perseverance. They'll seek the Lord with their entire being, in fulfillment of His words, "The kingdom of heaven suffers violence, and the violent take it by force" (Matthew 11:12).

The violent. What sort of company did Jesus envision with that designation? Let me be numbered with them! The lateness of the hour compels us toward violent abandonment. The signs of the times are increasing and Christ's return is growing more imminent. We must awaken from our stupor and chase down the kingdom of God with fresh fire and pounding urgency. With *violence*.

Authentic faith seeks God earnestly. "But without faith it is impossible to please Him, for he who comes to God must believe that He is, and that He is a rewarder of those who diligently seek Him" (Hebrews 11:6). Faith understands not only that God exists, but that He rewards us according to the intensity of our pursuit. God chasers exhibit their faith by the way they run. Men and women of faith won't be distracted from their objective because they know God rewards diligent seekers.

Spiritual violence begins in the secret place. It starts by avidly devoting ourselves to the disciplines of prayer, adoration, gazing, fasting, reading, study, meditation, listening, and absorbing truth. I say *absorbing truth* rather than *memorizing Scripture* because it's possible to memorize verses without the truth really penetrating our spirit, changing our lifestyle, and shaping our daily dialogue with God and people. I don't want to merely rattle off memory verses; I want truth living inwardly in me and manifesting outwardly in my daily walk.

One of the most violent things you'll do is wrestle down your schedule and carve time to shut yourself in with God. In busy seasons, it can seem like a thousand voices clamor for your attention. Which voice will rule—the loud voice of your to-do list, or the small voice that beckons to the secret place? *Swing your sword against the encroaching tentacles that seek to overgrow your secret life with God. Get alone with God, O man of violence! Kiss the Son, O woman of violence!*

Spiritual violence includes providing your body sufficient rest so that, when you get to the secret place, you're not too sleepy to connect with God. We exert violence the evening before so that the next morning is secured. I'm not suggesting the violent are never sleepy in the secret place, because we're human and we all have moments of nodding. God has plenty of room for our humanity. However, the violent wisely manage the rhythms of their schedule so they can be consistently alert and engaged during their most cherished part of the day.

We shouldn't confuse spiritual violence with natural zeal. Some people display spurts of zeal for God—perhaps in the way they worship or participate in church events. But natural zeal tends to last only while others are watching. When the buzz of activity is over and we're all alone, natural zeal tends to fizzle and collapse. Instead, we're reaching for true spiritual fervency—a Spirit-empowered zeal for Jesus that burns fiery-hot even when no one's looking.

A chapter on violence would fall short without speaking of *fasting*—the extraordinary tool God has given us to intensify the violence of our pursuit. Fasting, when combined with prayer, is one of the most effective ways to throw off sluggishness and accelerate the pace of our race.

Oh, what an awesome little gift this fasting thing is! It's probably one of the most under-rated, under-employed, under-appreciated gifts of grace. Now, there's no spiritual merit in fasting. It doesn't earn extra points with God. But it does tenderize your spirit, sensitize your hearing, and enhance your ability to receive the life of God. For those resolved to explore spiritual violence, fasting is a true friend. That's probably why Paul said he fasted *often* (2 Corinthians 11:27).

In Proverbs, Solomon portrayed godly wisdom as treasure buried deep in the rock. He said, "Seek [wisdom] as silver, and search for her as for hidden treasures" (Proverbs 2:4). To mine these nuggets you must tunnel fiercely for them. Furthermore, Daniel said that *God gives wisdom to the wise* (Daniel 2:21). In other words, the foolish don't receive the treasures of wisdom. Why not? Because they're too foolish to dig for them. Only those smart enough to go boring for hidden treasure are given these valuable nuggets. You have to go after them violently. That's where fasting comes in. Fasting, prayer, and word immersion help us drill down on the treasures of God that are hidden in Christ (Colossians 2:2-3).

Jesus doesn't respond to all believers alike. He's more responsive to those who seek more diligently. He meant so when He said, "With the measure you use, it will be measured back to you" (Matthew 7:2). For example, Jesus didn't respond equally to His twelve disciples. While He loved all twelve, He brought only three--Peter, James, and John—to some of His more significant moments. Was that because Jesus showed favoritism to the three? No. It was because there were different levels of abandonment among the twelve. While some held back in reservation (Matthew 28:17), Peter, James, and John pursued Jesus with greater abandonment. He didn't favor them because of their personalities or likeability; He favored them because they favored Him. Even among the twelve, the principle of Matthew 13:12 could be seen: Those who had more were given more.

I'm writing these things, dear friends, to inspire you

toward your Lord. Run after Him! Seek Him with all your heart! As you seek Him more fervently, He'll draw you closer than ever. Hold to His precious promise in 2 Chronicles 16:9, "For the eyes of the LORD run to and fro throughout the whole earth, to show Himself strong on behalf of those whose heart is loyal to Him."

The Lord is no respecter of persons. He rewards all according to the fervency of their pursuit. Those who don't seek much don't receive much. In accordance with 2 Corinthians 8:8, God compares the diligence of believers. For example, He sees the desperate diligence of a believer suffering in a prison for their faith and compares that with the sluggish softness of a rich believer in a prosperous nation who lacks for nothing. How could He possibly reward them equally?

1 Corinthians 9:24 reveals that we run our race in the presence of all the other saints: "Do you not know that those who run in a race all run, but one receives the prize? Run in such a way that you may obtain it." God honors our race as compared to how others have run throughout church history. Folks, we have some serious competition here. I do not mean that we compare our attainments with one another in a carnal way, but I mean that we allow the swiftness of other runners to inspire us toward greater pursuits in God.

I get inspired when I read the stories of the great Christian runners of history. I was stirred in my spirit when I read the story of how Francis of Assisi pursued God in his early twenties. One of his companions tells the story of how Francis crawled out of bed after he thought his companion was asleep. He knelt on the floor, and for the better part of the night prayed one single sentence: "My God and my all." Then he caught a little bit of sleep and awoke with the others. Such an intense pace!

I once read of a Chinese prisoner who fasted for 76 days from both food and water, praying for the salvation of his fellow prisoners who abused him the entire time. At the end of the 76 days, he arose in supernatural strength and authority, preached to his cellmates, and all fifteen of them repented on the spot. Wow!

I heard of some Chinese believers who were together on a 21-day fast because they hadn't seen anyone raised from the dead in three weeks, and they thought something was wrong.

And the stories go on and on. Oh, I love to be inspired by the violence of others!

As you read the following page from John Wesley's diary, you'll see a man who allowed nothing to daunt his pursuit of the high calling of God:

> Sunday Morning, May 5. Preached in St. Ann's. Was asked not to come back anymore.
>
> Sunday p.m., May 5. Preached at St. John's. Deacons said, "Get out and stay out."
>
> Sunday a.m., May 12. Preached at St. Jude's. Can't go back there either.
>
> Sunday p.m., May 12. Preached at St. George's. Kicked out again.
>
> Sunday a.m., May 19. Preached at St. somebody else's. Deacons called special meeting and said I couldn't return.
>
> Sunday p.m., May 19. Preached on the street. Kicked off the street.
>
> Sunday a.m., May 26. Preached in meadow, chased out of meadow as bull was turned loose during the service.
>
> Sunday a.m., June 2. Preached out at the edge of town, kicked off the highway.
>
> Sunday p.m., June 2, afternoon service. Preached in a pasture, 10,000 people came to hear me.

Go after God! No one else can hinder your race. It matters not whether other people recognize your ministry or maturity. Pursue the upward call of God in Christ! Choirs of saints are cheering you from the banisters of heaven. When you hear or read their stories in Scripture, their lives testify to us, "We finished the course by God's faithfulness and grace, and He will help you to run, too!"

Sacred history is laden with stories of men and women who ran a compelling race of faith, and we're given their stories to strengthen our faith and inspire our violence. These stories are the witness the author of Hebrews had in view when he wrote, "Therefore we also, since we are surrounded by so great a cloud of witnesses, let us lay aside every weight, and the sin which so easily ensnares us, and let us run with endurance the race that is set before us" (Hebrews 12:1).

Get back to the secret place, all you violent children of God!

CHAPTER TWELVE

The Secret of Humility

Our violent pursuit of God must be joined to a gentle and humble spirit. Humility is the foundation of all prayer. Humility says, *Lord, I'm empty without You; I'm broken without Your wholeness; I'm helpless without Your strength; I'm clueless without your wisdom. Apart from You I'm nothing. I need You! I need You so desperately that I've come to my secret place to pour my heart out to You. Again.*

Prayerlessness is the first sign of arrogance and independence. When we're feeling great, optimistic about our future, and confident in our path, we're often tempted to trim back our secret time with God. When we don't feel needy, it's a sign we're getting full of ourselves.

This morning, even before I knew I would be writing this chapter today, I was enjoying the words of Agur, who wrote, "Surely I am more stupid than any man, and do not have the understanding of a man. I neither learned wisdom nor have knowledge of the Holy One" (Proverbs 30:2-3). Agur's wisdom was to have a proper assessment of his own stupidity. Would to God we all owned that same awareness! It would drive us back to our knees, back to the source of all wisdom, back to God *who alone is wise* (Jude 1:25). If He alone is wise, where does that place us?

Once you see His immeasurable wealth and your utter bankruptcy, you're quick to humble yourself before Him. How eagerly the elders cast their crowns at the foot of the throne! They take the crown of their aggregate achievements and throw it all at the feet of Him from whom it all proceeded in the first place. He gave it to us that we might give it all back to Him. None of this was our idea. It all started with Him, happened through Him, and ends with Him (Romans 11:36).

As we're joined to Him, the poverty of our personal identity is lost in His eternal greatness.

David wrote, "O God, my heart is steadfast; I will sing and give praise, even with my glory" (Psalm 108:1). He was steadfast in his resolve to love the Lord in his secret place. He determined to praise the Lord *even with his glory*. What did he mean by that curious phrase? David's glory was the accumulated grandeur of all his attainments. What were some of his attainments? He had the glory of a world class king—majesty, wealth, honor, prestige, dignity, splendor, and power. He also had the distinction of being a sweet psalmist and an anointed prophet. He gathered the total of all God had given him and made of him, and gave it all back in songs of praise. The greater his prestige, the greater his joy in casting it before the majesty of He who gave it.

We have the same privilege. We gather ourselves, rise to the full height of all our life attainments, and cast it all at His feet because of His all-surpassing greatness. The greater our attainments (glory), the greater our joy in emptying it all before Him. That's the meaning of Psalm 108:1.

He enriches us that we might have something to lay before Him in humility and devotion. God dignifies us—with sonship, glory, acceptance, royalty, purpose, significance, wealth, honor, salvation, wisdom, revelation, understanding, status, character, holiness, victories—so that we might glory in the privilege of casting it all at His feet. We want a large crown so we have much to cast down.

And we're not waiting for the last day to do this. Like David, we're devoting ourselves *now* to the humility of worship. We go to the secret place—every day—to prostrate ourselves before His majesty and worship Him with our glory.

When David was criticized for abandoning his pride as he ministered to the Lord, he replied with these classic words, "I will play music before the Lord. And I will be even more undignified than this, and will be humble in my own sight"

(2 Samuel 6:21-22). Like David, God's servants realize that they're nothing and find no greater joy than searching ever-increasing ways to humble themselves in the presence of the Almighty One.

The secret place is where we acknowledge our spiritual bankruptcy, our need for mercy, and our dependence on Him for everything. We'll throw ourselves at His feet and we'll be even more undignified than this. How low can we go, and how high can we exalt Him?

CHAPTER THIRTEEN

The Secret of Intercession

Intercession is a powerful element in secret prayer, and functions primarily as *prayer on behalf of needs other than my own.* An intercessor is a priestly go-between. Standing between heaven's supply and earth's need, they beseech the Father for divine breakthrough.

The writer of Hebrews asked the saints to intercede on his behalf: "Pray for us; for we are confident that we have a good conscience, in all things desiring to live honorably. But I especially urge you to do this, that I may be restored to you the sooner" (Hebrews 13:18-19). He expected to visit them but indicated their intercession could speed his coming. If they would pray, he could get to them *sooner.* The secret is, *intercession accelerates God's purposes in the earth.*

Intercession has a way of *redeeming the time* (Ephesians 5:16) because we can actually buy time with our prayers. When evil is looming, we can postpone its coming; when good is delayed, we can accelerate its coming with our prayers.

God's purposes for this planet *are* going to happen. The question is not whether they'll happen; the question is, will we share in them? If we'll pray, God will work *sooner* in the earth and we'll have the thrill of participating. If we don't pray, God's purposes will happen—but perhaps in another generation.

I want in! That's why I intercede.

Jesus holds the keys to world history. He will open the seven seals of Revelation 5 at the time of His Father's choosing. When He does, world history will escalate toward its culmination and the age to come. God could wrap this whole thing up at any time, but He's looking for a generation that refuses to be bypassed—a generation that's so desperate to be included that they're giving themselves to incessant, insistent intercession.

One of the best ways to love someone is to pray for them. When you do, you invest in that person's life. Even if you don't approve of everything they're doing, intercession will join your heart to theirs in affection. As you intercede for someone, you can't help but fall in love with them all over again. Here's the secret: Intercessory prayers become *cords of affection* that bind the hearts of believers to one another. Prayer joins the body of Christ together in the greatest of all virtues—love.

Paul loved the saints in Corinth dearly, but it wasn't enough that he felt that love on the inside. He wanted *them* to feel and see his love—to *know the love which I have so abundantly for you* (2 Corinthians 2:4). He wanted his love for them to *appear* to them (2 Corinthians 7:12). With Paul's example in mind, how can we help others see how much we love them? One way would be by telling them, "I've been praying for you." When you say that to someone, it helps them *feel* and *know* your love for them.

The community of faith functions properly only when its members are praying for one another. *Prayer is the immunity system of the body of Christ.* Through prayer, we fight off the invasive forces that seek to disease and afflict the church of Jesus Christ.

Prayerlessness in the body of Christ is akin to leprosy. According to Paul Brand, a surgeon to lepers, leprosy causes nerves to stop functioning properly. Body parts that are leprous will stop sending pain signals to the brain. As a result, lepers will injure those members without even realizing it. Eventually, they'll lose fingers and toes through abrasions because they didn't even realize they were hurting themselves.

In a similar way, when believers are hurt but the church feels no pain, it indicates the presence of *spiritual leprosy*. The church's nerves are dead. Next, the church begins to lose body members.

Pain signals the body to send help to the hurting member. Pain is essential if the body is to repair and heal itself. Thus, *pain is a gift* because it compels us to tend to hurting members. Prayer is one way we help our wounded. We cry out in intercession for deliverance and grace because we're in pain over a need in the body of Christ.

Intercession is a response to pain. Just as someone with a broken arm will cry out painfully for help, we cry out in prayer when a member in the body of Christ is broken.

As I think on these things, I'm reminded of friends who face chronic illnesses and incurable medical conditions. Saints in desperate health straits send an urgent message to the body of Christ: *The church is sick. We lack the power to heal this member. Danger! Alert! We must rally and do everything possible for this member to be healed.* In the face of such distress, however, too often the church is distant and unfeeling. We don't always feel the intensity of a sick member's suffering. Do we have spiritual leprosy? Are we prayerless?

When we're healthy, we *remember the prisoners as if chained with them* (Hebrews 13:3). Their suffering is our suffering. This kind of healthy pain moves us to pray with renewed passion and intensity.

In your secret place, ask the Lord to tenderize you with feelings of affection for your needy brothers and sisters. Then ask Him to help you direct those holy affections into intercession. Love is the secret to intercession. Love is meant to flow and intercession is meant to be fiery.

Love, drive us to our knees. Holy Spirit, help us feel Your urgency for the cause before us. Give us answered prayer! We'll never relent until we see a release of the overcoming authority that Jesus died to give us.

CHAPTER FOURTEEN

The Secret of Watching

Jesus connected prayer with vigilant watching. Twice He told His disciples, *Watch and pray* (Mark 13:33; 14:38), because prayer has to do with the eyes. Prayer is wide-eyed, attentive, and fully alert. In the secret place, we're not hiding from current events like an ostrich burying its head in the sand; rather, we're holding our circumstances before the search light of the Scriptures and the Holy Spirit.

Pray with eyes wide open.

Jesus exhorted us to watch for His second coming:

> But of that day and hour no one knows, not even the angels in heaven, nor the Son, but only the Father. Take heed, watch and pray; for you do not know when the time is. It is like a man going to a far country, who left his house and gave authority to his servants, and to each his work, and commanded the doorkeeper to watch. Watch therefore, for you do not know when the master of the house is coming—in the evening, at midnight, at the crowing of the rooster, or in the morning—lest, coming suddenly, he find you sleeping. And what I say to you, I say to all: Watch! (Mark 13:32-37).

You just read one of Jesus' most urgent exhortations. He couldn't have been clearer. He was heralding believers of all time to constant, vigilant, clear-eyed alertness. For what should we watch and pray? For the return of our Lord.

One pastor was asked how many people come to his church. He replied, "Oh, we sleep 800." Sadly, too many believers are asleep in the most momentous hour of human history.

The Lord never placed on us the burden of seeing into the future. He does expect us, though, to be alert to the hour in which we live and to discern the signs of our time.

I know only one way to fulfill this urgent mandate: By praying faithfully in secret. In the secret place:

- We sharpen our spiritual senses to heaven's whispers
- We discern current events through the lens of God's word
- We detect the themes and portions of Scripture the Spirit is currently emphasizing
- We calibrate our souls to the straight ways of the Lord
- We quiet our hearts long enough to listen
- We gaze with rapt attention upon the throne of God
- We put away spiritual slumber, sluggishness, and distractions
- We're ignited and renewed in love

An important word in this hour is *discernment.* Jesus wants us discerning the signs of the times. Discernment is developed, not by reading online news, but by reading God's word. That's where we learn what His voice sounds like. We stand at attention to watch His every move. We search out the wisdom that discerns the mystery of iniquity and the mystery of godliness in the earth today.

Sometimes, in my secret place, I put everything else aside (such as reading or requests), and pause to ask Him questions. *Lord, what are You doing in the earth today? What themes are You emphasizing right now? Among which groups of people are You moving in a special way? What do You want me to see concerning the day and hour in which I live? What is my role in Your present activities?* Then I wait upon Him for insight and understanding. I desire to be alert to the things most dear to God's heart in this present hour. This is why I knock, wait, and watch.

Jesus said, "Behold, I am coming as a thief. Blessed is he who watches" (Revelation 16:15). When a thief visits, he'll sometimes give off small signals of his approach—the turning of a latch, the sound of a footstep, a bump into an unseen object, etc. Similarly, there will be subtle signs of Christ's coming which only the alert will notice. Only those who watch and pray will discern the sounds of His footsteps. What a blessing to be found on active duty and alert at His coming!

Here's another important end-time exhortation from Jesus:

> Let your waist be girded and your lamps burning; and you yourselves be like men who wait for their master, when he will return from the wedding, that when he comes and knocks they may open to him immediately. Blessed are those servants whom the master, when he comes, will find watching. Assuredly, I say to you that he will gird himself and have them sit down to eat, and will come and serve them. And if he should come in the second watch, or come in the third watch, and find them so, blessed are those servants. But know this, that if the master of the house had known what hour the thief would come, he would have watched and not allowed his house to be broken into. Therefore you also be ready, for the Son of Man is coming at an hour you do not expect (Luke 12:35-40).

In the garden of prayer we arouse from sleep, gird our waist for action, and trim the lamps of our love so they burn bright. To stay ready for the imminent return of your Lover and Friend, watch and pray.

The secret place is *the* place to watch for Christ's return. When Jesus prayed in Gethsemane, all He wanted His disciples to do was *watch*. Prayer has to do with the *eyes*—with the way we focus our attention. Get in the secret place, open your eyes, and watch.

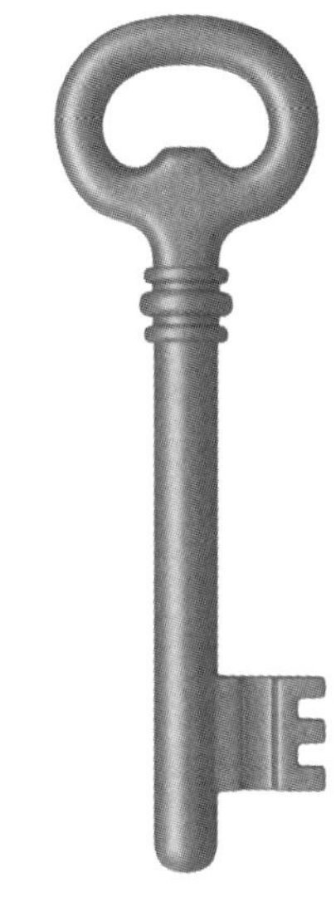

PART II

Making It Work

In the last section, we covered foundational principles that inspire us to establish a secret place relationship with the Lord. Now, let's look at some practical tools that will help us maximize our moments and find a cadence with Jesus that really works for us.

CHAPTER FIFTEEN

The Secret of Radiation Therapy

All believers struggle to overcome sin. Scripture describes this conflict as *striving against sin* (Hebrews 12:4). Some are further ahead in this struggle than others. Some believers carry more baggage from their old life of sin, making the fight to overcome seem more intense. Whatever your level of victory over sin, you probably wish at times that you could enjoy even greater victory.

How do we overcome sinful patterns? The pathway would probably include such things as repentance, renouncing of old habits, the cleansing of the blood of Jesus, prayers of agreement, accountability, forgiveness, self-denial, etc. However, I want to focus in this chapter on one secret to overcoming sin that is sometimes overlooked. I call it, *exposing ourselves to the radiation of God's presence.*

Sin is like a cancer; God's presence is like radiation on that cancer. The longer you're in His presence, ingesting His word and basking in His glory, the more overcoming power you're absorbing into your soul. When God's presence gains greater sway over your life, sin's power diminishes.

The longer we expose our wayward hearts to the presence of His glory, the smaller the tumors of sin become. We need time exposures to glory.

The presence of Jesus is the place of change. Distancing ourselves from God always produces spiritual regression; proximity to God always produces spiritual progress. You can usually distinguish between conviction and condemnation by looking at the direction the voice is compelling you—toward or away from the Lord. The agenda of *condemnation's* voice is to push you *away from* His presence—away from that which is the very source of your victory. The purpose of *conviction's* voice is to press you *into* the face of Christ where victory is accessed. Listen to Holy Spirit conviction, not demonic condemnation. Draw close to God!

In Moses' day, God always wanted to get close to His people but, whenever He did, people died. The Old Testament saga of the exodus from Egypt unfolds the gripping story of how a yearning God came close to His people, only to be confronted with their blatant unbelief and disobedience. God's fiery holiness couldn't allow for outright rebellion and transgression. If God was to stay, the rebels had to go. To the consternation of all involved, when God and people lived together, people died. What was to be done?

At Mount Sinai, God's solution was to admonish the people to keep their distance (Exodus 19:12-13, 21-24). But God's presence in the camp continued to be deadly to thousands of people. So many were dying in the wilderness that eventually the people said to Moses, "Surely we die, we perish, we all perish! Whoever even comes near the tabernacle of the LORD must die. Shall we all utterly die?" (Numbers 17:12-13). God was also aware of the problem, for He said to them, "I will not go up in your midst, lest I consume you on the way" (Exodus 33:3). According to Deuteronomy 5:25-27, the people told Moses they would die if they came close to God, so they asked Moses to draw near to God on their behalf. God agreed that Moses should draw near and the people should keep their distance (Deuteronomy 5:28).

But there was a fatal flaw here. If they would draw near to God's presence—to receive strength for greater faith and obedience—many would be killed. If they would keep their distance from God's glory in order to survive, they would spiral into greater unbelief and disobedience. It was a lose-lose situation. They had to maintain their distance in order to survive, but their distance from God caused them to deteriorate into further sin—which in turn required that they maintain a greater distance. This vicious downward cycle was a hopeless spiral that only God Himself could remedy. The solution, ultimately, was in the cross of Christ.

Yes! The cross! Now, through the blood of Calvary, sinful people are able to come into the immediate presence of God's holiness and be changed by exposing themselves to God's glory. When we hide nothing from His light, we're transformed into the likeness of Christ (2 Corinthians 3:18).

The access we now have because of Christ's blood is utterly amazing. We're still weak and sinful, and yet we're able to come into the immediate presence of His Holiness. What a privilege! Only a fool would neglect or avoid this place of glorious change and delightful intimacy. God has killed Himself (literally) to bring us into His presence.

When we step into God's presence, we're exposing ourselves to *power*. Everything within us changes when we bask in the radiation of His glory.

The sun provides our planet with heat, light, energy, and ultraviolet rays—radiation. In a similar way, God warms our lives. Psalm 84:11 actually calls God *a sun*. Like planets circling the sun, our lives revolve around God, soaking up the power that radiates from Him. When we place ourselves before the radiation of His countenance, His glory does violence to cancerous iniquities.

Do you have pockets of sin you struggle to overcome? Let me tell you what to do. Expose yourself to God's radiation. If you do, you'll be amazed at the traction you'll gain over chronic sin issues that have plagued you.

Time in His presence is possibly the most potent antidote to habitual, recurring sins.

You don't know you're exposed to radiation when it first happens. For example, sunburned people don't always realize they're getting too many rays until after the damage is done. That's because radiation's effects are somewhat delayed. The same is true of God's glory. When you spend time in His presence and don't feel an immediate difference, you may be tempted to think, *This isn't accomplishing anything*. However, if you'll continue to devote mega-amounts of time to His presence, the effects of spending time with Him will eventually manifest.

I speak from personal experience when I say that *powerful things happen on the inside when you spend time with God*. The molecular composition of your soul gets restructured. You start to think differently and may not even be able to pinpoint why. Your passions, interests, and instinctive responses change. You probably won't be able to analyze it completely, but you'll realize you're changing from the inside out. Sinful affections that once pulled at your soul no longer have power over you. The secret is simply this: You've learned the transformational power of spending chunks of time in God's presence—loving Him and receiving His word.

One last thought and this chapter is done. On Mount Sinai, Moses lived in God's immediate glory for eighty days. How did he survive? Wouldn't eighty days give him a radiation overdose? Clearly, God shielded him to some extent so he could survive the exposure. Here's my question, therefore: Is it possible to build up an ability to handle heavier exposures to the glory of God? As in the case of Moses, I think the answer is yes. The more time you spend in His presence, the greater your ability to steward and sustain even greater levels of glory. Would it be okay to say that you begin to develop a *Son-tan*?

If I can use the image of a Son-tan, I would view it like a mark of time spent with Him. A tan enables us to spend even more time in the sun's radiation without being burned. Jesus said it this way: "To everyone who has, more will be given, and he will have abundance" (Matthew 25:29). Spend time in His presence and He'll take you on an adventure of being changed *from glory to glory* (2 Corinthians 3:18).

Makes you want to run into the secret place, doesn't it?

CHAPTER SIXTEEN

The Secret of Time

A friend told me, "The secret place has been the point of greatest frustration and attack in my personal walk." He's not alone. The secret place holds the keys to the overcoming life, so the enemy will focus his strongest assaults on this area of our lives.

Our enemy will do *anything* to get us to curtail the amount of secret time we devote to God. He'll squeeze, distract, harass, incite, oppress, entice, weary, intimidate—whatever it takes. Make no mistake, when you devote yourself to knowing God, all hell will seemingly rise up to distract you.

To find the potential of the secret place requires one pivotal element: *time.* Lots of it. The more exclusive time you give Him, the more meaningful the relationship. The principle of 2 Corinthians 9:6 applies here, "He who sows sparingly will also reap sparingly, and he who sows bountifully will also reap bountifully." Sow more time to the secret place and you'll enjoy a corresponding bounty.

To uncover the full joy of the secret place, there's a threshold to cross. Until you cross that threshold, you may find that you have to push yourself to get alone with God. But once you cross the threshold, the secret place loses any sense of burden and instead carries a newfound sense of delight. With joy, you'll gladly prioritize it even under the pressure of other competing demands.

How do we find that threshold? By giving *time* to the secret place. I never consider time invested in the secret place a waste; and even if it is, I gladly waste it upon my Lord! Even when we feel like we're spinning our wheels spiritually, every hour invested is filling up prayer bowls in the Spirit (Revelation 5:8).

One day the bowl will reach the tipping point, and the Lord will take us through the threshold into another dimension of delight and intimacy. But we'll never get there without investing time.

Another friend told me she had feelings of guilt over not taking enough time to be with the Lord. This is a common feeling, but it's seriously misdirected. Feelings of guilt never motivated anyone to spend more time with God; in actuality, they discourage us and make us feel like failures. Rather than fuel our fire, guilt can potentially snuff out whatever flame we might have.

Guilt is founded on lies. Satan wants you to believe that God is disappointed with you because you haven't been meeting your daily quota of time with Him. The truth is, your acceptance with God has to do with only one thing—your faith in Christ. God is very unimpressed with your ability to performance spirituality, but He's deeply impressed with Christ's performance on the cross. When you put childlike faith in Christ's redemptive work, His performance is credited to you. Faith in Christ unlocks the Father's heart to you. When you believe in His beloved Son, the Father's heart explodes in affirmation, acceptance, and delight—independently of your spiritual diligence or lack thereof.

God is your greatest fan. As your heavenly Father, He's constantly coaxing and coaching you forward toward greater spiritual victory. When you neglect the secret place, He's not disappointed *in* you, He's disappointed *for* you. He knows the riches that could be yours, and His heart yearns when He sees you being deprived. He wants you to share in heaven's best, and He's pained when you short-change yourself spiritually.

Someone once said to me, *The greatest lie Satan attacks me with is, "You deserve a break today!"* Some of Satan's lies are so stupid they're literally ridiculous. *As though time away from the secret place is a break!* It's not a break, it's a loss. You missed drinking deeply of the Spirit's fountain; you missed being washed and cleansed and renewed in His presence; you missed getting fed by the richness of God's word; you missed taking the time to calm your hectic heart and hear His precious voice; you missed the intimate communion of the secret garden. As the saying goes, *You was robbed.*

When Satan tricks you into skipping your secret place, instead of feeling guilty, you should feel *ripped off!* When circumstances or emotions successfully rob your secret place, *don't get guilty—get indignant!* Let *lovesickness* take you over. *Oh Lord, I love You so much. I'm really upset at the way I've allowed the cares of this life to crowd You out. This has to stop, things have got to change. I can't live without You. I'm coming back! I've got to have more time with You. You are my life, my breath. I love You, Lord!* And then exert spiritual violence to get your priorities back in line.

On a practical note, many who have found great joy in their secret life with God have found it necessary to devote a specific portion of the day to meeting with Him. Although it requires discipline, devoting ourselves consistently to the same time slot daily can be helpful in finding a higher dimension. When we relegate the secret place entirely to spontaneity, in retrospect we usually find that we didn't end up giving it much time. Find the balance between discipline and spontaneity that works for you. In the end, we want to develop patterns that enable us to be devoted to long and loving meditation on the wonders of Christ Jesus.

Here's another practical tip: *Work your way slowly to spending more time with Him.* If you're doing ten minutes a day right now, make it fifteen or twenty. By adding incrementally, you'll build spiritual stamina. Spiritual stamina doesn't come naturally to us. For example, I was once with a brother who was wanting to devote himself to prayer and study regarding a specific struggle in his life. I noticed, however, that after giving himself to the study for a few minutes, he had to quit and move on to something else. He hadn't yet developed an ability to endure in prayer and the word. Even a mere half-hour of study and prayer was too long for his attention span. It was almost as though he had *Spiritual Attention Deficit Disorder*. He was at a crossroads where God was inviting him to mature and develop the ability to spend more time in the secret place. If you'll accept the Lord's challenge to stay with it and add time in small increments, over time you'll develop spiritual endurance.

Train for it like an athlete. No athlete expects to run a marathon their first time out. If they're stepping out of a sedentary lifestyle, a runner needs time to build endurance. Every day they add a little more until they're able to endure for the desired period. Similarly, you can build your endurance until spending extended time with Him is your delight.

When I think of running this race, I think of Psalm 119:32, "I will run the course of Your commandments, for You shall enlarge my heart." A runner must develop strength of heart. As they push themselves to run further—faster—the heart's ability to pump blood through the entire body is enlarged. Similarly, I want the Lord to enlarge my *spiritual heart* that I might be able to spend longer time periods with Him.

We're not finished with this theme yet. Come to the next chapter and let me talk about a specific way we can plan more time alone with God.

CHAPTER SEVENTEEN

The Secret of Retreats

Nothing can replace a consistent secret life with God, but there is something that can augment it: *prayer retreats*. I want to talk about how they can strengthen our prayer lives.

I've found personal prayer retreats helpful in several ways:

- They intensify and accelerate my pursuit of God.
- They refresh and renew my spirit.
- They sharpen my responsiveness to receive revelation from God.
- They've helped me receive divine guidance for specific situations.
- God has honored them by revealing hidden things.
- They've increased my understanding of God's ways and works.
- When I've not known how I would continue, they've kept me alive spiritually.

Because of these benefits, I've become a strong advocate of prayer retreats. I'm going to do my best to win you to their wisdom. This chapter will have been successful if I can motivate you to schedule them into your calendar.

A friend of mine, Kelly, has the practice of scheduling a prayer retreat once a year. He reserves a room at a retreat facility, camp, or hotel, and sets aside three full days to be alone with God. Either he selects a long holiday weekend or takes a Friday off from work to lengthen the weekend. These fasting retreats have become so fruitful in his walk with God that he's determined to do them annually. I've noticed other believers will watch his consecration, admire the fruit in his life, but yet never take the plunge themselves. It leaves me sad and perplexed. Why don't more Christians do this?

Effective retreats wisely include four elements: solitude, no entertainment, fasting, and the Gospels.

- Solitude: Group retreats are useful in their own way, but I'm talking about getting alone with God. The quieter the better. Isolate from the everyday demands of life. Shut yourself in, except perhaps for outdoor prayer walks. Curtail texts and communications to an absolute minimum. Face the loneliness head-on. You may be struck with the way social interaction has anesthetized your awareness of God. The violent separation from all distractions is vital to maximizing your retreat time.
- No entertainment: This means no phone or device distractions, no TV, videos, radio, newspapers, computer games, social media, etc. Part of the intensity of the retreat will derive from your refusal to medicate the boredom of being with no one else or nothing else but God. You'll eventually move past it, but initially the boredom will reveal things in your heart the Spirit wants to confront.
- Fasting: Fasting frees you from the distraction of food preparation and consumption. It also intensifies your pursuit of God through the grace that accompanies self-denial. The more austere your fast, the stronger the benefit. A water-only fast is more violent than a juice-only fast. If your health allows it, I recommend a water-only fast except for the Lord's Supper daily. I suggest you wean yourself off caffeine before the retreat begins.
- The Gospels: Fill your retreat with meditations from a wide variety of Scriptures, but go hard and heavy on

> readings in the Gospels. *Read the red.* Let Jesus Himself hold your heart during these precious moments. By all means be prepared to journal because the Lord is about to give you download at a rate you've not known in quite a while.

If you decide to carve a three-day retreat into your schedule, watch and see how the Lord helps you pull it off. To pastors and spiritual leaders who enjoy the privilege of having their full-time employment in the work of God, however, I am recommending a step further. By all means, start with a three-day retreat. But work your way up to even more. I would highly commend a seven-day or ten-day retreat once a year. And for some, even more. Here's why.

Chances are that the first one or two days of your retreat will be filled with above-average quantities of sleep and extra fog. That's okay, you'll need the sleep to be renewed and to clear the cobwebs. By the end of the third day, it's common to feel like, "I'm just now starting to gain some spiritual momentum." And you're right. I've discovered that the real momentum doesn't kick in until the fifth or sixth day. Around day six you break free of the barrier reef. Go on a ten-day water-only retreat and experience what I mean by that.

I'm saddened with the awareness that most of you reading this will not believe these words enough to actually do them. But I'm writing for those who have ears to hear. If you can receive it, I am truthfully pointing you to one of the greatest secrets of the secret place. Your secret life can be lifted to new levels with God through the strategic employment of prayer and fasting retreats at planned intervals throughout the journey.

Fasting retreats have made the difference in my spiritual survival. That's why I'm so passionate about this. I stumbled onto this means of grace in an unexpected way, and now I wish I could persuade all my brothers and sisters of this wisdom.

Never done it before? That's okay. Just jump in. You have an awesome teacher with you—the Holy Spirit. He'll guide you into all truth. You don't need a human helper or mentor to teach you about this, the Holy Spirit Himself will show you the way. He'll fit you with a yoke that wears perfectly for you. Grab your calendar and schedule it, right now, into your upcoming year.

CHAPTER EIGHTEEN

The Secret of Journaling

I am fiercely committed to keeping a spiritual journal because it helps me retain the insights God gives me in His word. I want to hold on to every word He gives, and here's why: *Those who retain what God gives them will be given more.* Jesus is the one who articulated this truth:

> Take heed how you hear. For whoever has, to him more will be given (Luke 8:18).

The linchpin word in the verse is *how*. Jesus advised us to be careful *how* we hear God's word. Why? Because if we receive His word in such a way that we labor to understand it, believe it, retain it, cherish it, live it, and make it part of our eternal history, He'll give us more.

The principle of Luke 8:18 is this: To receive a fresh word from God, I must prove myself a faithful steward of the last word He gave me.

Suppose God spoke a powerful word to me at one time, and then He comes a couple years later to check and see what I've been doing with it. Two years later, He finds that it's fallen off my radar, it's dusty, mostly neglected, and I've all but forgotten it. His response is likely to be something like, *If that's how you valued the last word I gave you, why should I give you another?* If I want Him to speak another life-changing word to my heart, I must demonstrate that the last word He gave me was so precious to me that I did everything in my power to retain it and live it.

This principle from Jesus is important to me for one simple reason: *I want more!* I want more revelation into the majesty of Christ. I want more faith and love. According to Jesus, the way to be given more is to prove myself a faithful steward of what He's already given.

I see an illustration of this principle in American football. In football, much of the game depends upon the receiver catching and holding on to the football. When the quarterback throws the ball, if the receiver catches and retains it, the game advances. But if the receiver tries to catch the ball but then drops it, the game goes all the way back to the former position.

To be appointed a receiver on a football team, you must have a consistent track record of catching footballs. If you keep on dropping balls, the quarterback will stop passing the ball to you. But if you keep catching balls, the quarterback will throw you more. This is the principle of Luke 8:18. *Catch the words Jesus throws you and He'll throw you more.*

I want to catch every football (word) Jesus throws my way because I want Him to throw me even more. So I've devised a system for catching footballs (scriptural insights) He throws me. To understand my system, you must know something about me: I have a horrible memory. Yours is probably great, but mine is like a sieve. If a thought comes to me that I want to remember, I have to write it down. If I don't write it down, it will take wings like a bird and be gone. The only way I can retain any insights the Holy Spirit throws my way is by writing them down. I call it *journaling.*

To retain a football Jesus throws me, I've got to write that word into my journal and then review it. I do this to compensate for my weak memory. It's not enough to just write it in my journal; I must then review my journal. If I write something in my journal but then never review it, it will fly away. My personal secret to retaining the words of Christ is to record them and then review them systematically.

When I speak of a journal, I'm not talking about a personal diary. I don't mean making entries such as, "Susan came over to visit. We had breakfast together and then went shopping." No, I'm thinking of something more consequential. Make your journal the place where you chronicle the spiritual truths that quicken your heart while you're in the secret place. When God feeds you with His manna, write it down. And later, review. Keep visiting that truth until it's woven into the fabric of your Christian experience and conduct.

My journal helps me hold onto footballs by giving me a way to revisit the things God has given me. I know that as I'm faithful to hold onto this football, He'll throw me another.

If a paper journal works best for you, go with it. For me, I like to keep my journal in my computer. I prefer to use a computer because once the scriptural meditation is in a digital format, it's easy to edit, copy/paste into other files, and share with others. I also copy journal entries into my topical library, which consists of individual text files organized by topic (such as faith, love, humility, etc.). Those topical files are like a portable library that travels with me inside my laptop.

I've made the psalmist's vow my personal ambition: "I will not forget Your word" (Psalm 119:16). When He feeds me with insight from His word, I labor with all my soul to retain that truth. How? Here's the secret: write it down, and then review.

Do not drop the ball!

CHAPTER NINETEEN

The Secret of Meditating

> This Book of the Law shall not depart from your mouth, but you shall meditate in it day and night, that you may observe to do according to all that is written in it. For then you will make your way prosperous, and then you will have good success (Joshua 1:8).

What does it mean to meditate in God's word? It means to slow down the reading pace and contemplate every word and phrase, looking for deeper and richer meanings. We meditate to mine the hidden treasures of God's word. The Scriptures are like a mountain range with vast pockets of jewels and veins of gold. The secret place is where we dig. We ponder and turn the phrases over and over in order to uncover the many layers of meaning within each word. I always assume that every verse has more significance to it than I have yet discovered. Meditation is the art of digging for that *hidden manna* (Revelation 2:17).

The written word of God is revealed by the Living Word, through the power of the Holy Spirit. "From His mouth come knowledge and understanding" (Proverbs 2:6). The source of illumination is Christ's mouth. As we meditate in His word, we get in the Spirit and then cry from our hearts, "*Lord, talk to me!*" We realize that without His help we'll never unlock the magnificent riches of His word.

Every word of Scripture can sustain the scrutiny of rigorous inquiry. When we search the word intensely for fresh insight, we're practicing Psalm 77:6—"I meditate within my heart, and my spirit makes diligent search."

There's much more depth to Scripture than what meets the eye at first reading. Some truths will never be found until you take the time to sit and stare at the text, mulling the message and its implications. Apparent contradictions or paradoxes sometimes contain the greatest truths. Some passages have multiple applications, containing layers of truth that are uncovered almost like the peeling of an onion.

A great way to meditate in God's word is to ask questions of the text. What does the verse say, and why? What does it mean? What other verses shed light on this one? What is the verse *not* saying? Does the verse contain a spiritual principle? How does this truth apply to my life?

Keep at it and you'll develop your own way of asking questions of the text. One of my favorite questions is, *Why did the Holy Spirit choose to word it this way?* Why did He use this word or phrase when He could have said it differently? When a phrase appears to make no contribution to the passage, I'll gaze on it and wonder why it was included. When a verse appears oblique or mysterious, my curiosity gets aroused. And when a verse seems overly obvious, I become suspicious that there may be depths of truth to it that I could easily overlook.

Here are some ways to ask questions of a text as you meditate.

- **Context:**
  A verse is usually understood better by examining the verses that precede and follow it. How do the previous verses set a backdrop for this verse? How do the verses following bring clarity and fuller understanding?
- **Word meanings:**
  Some of the words in the original Bible languages of Hebrew and Greek carry more than one possible meaning. What various shades of meaning do the significant words in this verse contain? Will other Bible translations provide colorful facets of meaning? Will Bible reference materials such as a Bible Dictionary or Commentary give further insight?
- **Cross-references:**
  While meditating in a verse, you can use a Bible Concordance or Bible software to find other verses that

contain the same words, phrases, or concepts. That other verse might put an interesting slant on the verse you're studying. To do this even faster, find a *Reference Edition Bible* with cross-references appearing as footnotes.

- **Repetition:**
  What words deserve extra attention because of their recurrence? Can I discover truths the Scriptures may be highlighting by looking for repeated words or concepts?
- **Symbolism:**
  What word pictures are being used? What do the word pictures represent? Do symbols in the text point to deeper spiritual meanings?

As you meditate in God's word, you'll slowly replenish the contents of your inner well. As Jesus said, "A good man out of the good treasure of his heart brings forth good; and an evil man out of the evil treasure of his heart brings forth evil. For out of the abundance of the heart his mouth speaks" (Luke 6:45). All of us have had deposits of *evil treasure* within; but in word meditation, those deposits are replaced with *good treasure*. In the secret place, we're squirreling away good treasure. Good displaces evil, just as light dispels darkness. As you absorb goodness internally, your actions and speech change externally. You're becoming more Christlike!

Once you come alive to meditating in God's word, you'll become addicted to the words of His mouth. The secret place will become your favorite place—better than a podcast, sermon, book, or conference. Why? Because it's where Jesus feeds you personally. This is where we glean the sweetest morsels. When you hear a sermon, you're listening to someone else's insights in the word; but in the secret place, you're receiving insights from Jesus that are custom made just for you. You don't have to imagine how that word applies to your life because *it comes with your name on it*. It nails where you're living. It sustains your spirit, flushes your cheeks, and puts fresh light in your eyes, because it's a word straight from His mouth to your heart. Personalized words from the Scriptures have the power, through the Holy Spirit, to sustain and carry you through life's greatest trials. This is the true fountain of life!

Proverbs 16:26 says, "The person who labors, labors for himself, for his hungry mouth drives him on." That verse describes the spiritual hunger that drives us into the secret place. When we're revived and fed by His word, we develop an appetite for more. (Because healthy sheep have a healthy appetite.) We've tasted the sweetness of His mouth and now we're ruined. Addicted. We want more!

Feeding on God's word only makes you hungrier. Now that you've tasted, you'll do anything to receive more of His words. You're no longer coming to the secret place from a sense of duty; rather, you run with longing into the secret place because you've become desperate for more. Your hungry mouth is literally driving you on.

When you awaken to the pleasure of sitting at His feet and meditating in His word, the secret place becomes your all-time favorite occupation in life.

Here's the secret:

> Finally, brethren, whatever things are true, whatever things are noble, whatever things are just, whatever things are pure, whatever things are lovely, whatever things are of good report, if there is any virtue and if there is anything praiseworthy—meditate on these things (Philippians 4:8).

CHAPTER TWENTY

The Secret of Simultaneous Reading

Reading Scripture in a spirit of eager submission to God is dramatically life-transforming. The power of His word changes us! Revelation 1:3 pronounces a blessing upon its readers. *All you have to do to be blessed is read the book.* Those who understand this are firmly committed to daily Bible reading.

Additionally, we are assured that, "All Scripture is given by inspiration of God and is profitable" (2 Timothy 3:16). In other words, every portion of the Bible is profitable to the reader. If we're eager to be conformed to the image of Christ, no portion of Scripture should be bypassed or overlooked. We discover more about the glory of who He is literally on every page.

Therefore, it behooves us to read the Bible in its entirety. I've been reading through the Bible annually for many years, and am committed to this practice because *I want every single portion of God's word to have a chance at my heart.* I don't want a single issue in my soul to remain unmoved because I failed to expose myself to the full breadth of His wisdom and revelation. I want the full package, so I read the full package.

Bible reading is much more than simply fulfilling a daily quota. We're not going, "Whew, I'm finally finished with today's reading; now I can get on with life." Not at all. Time in the word is our place of renewal, sustenance, and change. Therefore, we're zealous to expose our hearts consistently and routinely to every living, breathing, inspired portion of Scripture.

Someone once said the most frequently read book of the Bible is Genesis. That's because thousands of people adopt a New Year's resolution to read through the Bible that year.

They'll launch into the book of Genesis but lose momentum along the way. Perhaps they get bogged down or bored when they get to Leviticus. But I know a secret that keeps me from getting bogged down in my Bible reading, and I'm going to share it in this chapter.

One of the best ways to maintain momentum in daily Bible reading, at least in my experience, is the secret of simultaneous reading. Instead of doing a lengthy reading in just one Bible book, I advocate reading shorter portions in a few different Bible books on the same day. This could be done in various ways, but let me illustrate by explaining my personal regimen of Bible reading.

I divide my Bible into four sections and read daily in each of these sections:

- Genesis to Malachi
- Psalms/Proverbs
- Matthew to John
- Acts to Revelation

I count how many pages are in each section, and then calculate how many pages to read daily to complete that section in a year. I don't read a set number of *chapters* each day but rather a set number of *pages*.

Then I find a way to mark where I left off. When using a paper Bible, I use paper clips to mark my locations. When using an eBook on an electronic reader, I use the device's Bookmark function.

I like to read annually through the Old Testament (Genesis to Malachi), so I count the number of pages in my Bible's Old Testament (excluding Psalms and Proverbs). Then, I divide that number by 300 to determine the number of pages I want to read daily. (I divide by 300, even though there are 365 days in a year, to allow for missed days.) If my Bible has, let's say,

3,000 pages in the Old Testament, then I'll aim to read 10 pages a day (10 pages times 300 days equals 3,000). This system works identically for both paper and electronic Bibles.

Next, I like to read through Psalms and Proverbs once a year. A bookmark reminds me where I left off.

Next, I read through the Gospels annually (Matthew to John). In fact, in this case I aim for twice a year because I personally like to read the New Testament twice annually. Using the same math process, I calculate how many pages to read daily to reach my goal. A bookmark keeps track of my progress.

Finally, I calculate how many pages to read daily if I'm to read twice annually through the Epistles (Acts to Revelation). And I mark my spot each day.

The number of pages you read in each section will depend upon your own personal reading goals. You can decide to read through a certain section of Scripture once a year, twice a year, once every two years, or whatever you want.

I want to express how I enjoy each of the four sections.

Genesis to Malachi: The Old Testament has both riveting stories and harder-to-read sections. When I get in a portion that feels mundane to read, I don't get bogged down because I'll also have readings that day in the New Testament. By persevering in the tough passages, I've discovered something: *The tough passages get a little bit easier to follow each time because I'm slowly growing in understanding with each reading.* Furthermore, when we think we're in the dreariest passage imaginable, the Lord has an uncanny way of unexpectedly downloading something that brings our heart alive. The most remote passages sometimes contain some of the sweetest surprises.

Psalms/Proverbs: When I come to Psalms, *my pace of reading slows way down.* These are the Bible's love songs and they give me language for prayer. Much of my secret place time is spent luxuriantly wending my way through the prayers and praises of the psalmists. Here I freely give the Lord the tender affections of my heart.

Matthew to John: I *love* this third section! *It's in the Gospels that I behold my Beloved.* I watch how He moves, acts, talks, thinks. My heart aches to know Him better and behold Him more clearly. The motivation for immersing myself in the Gospels derives from Jesus' promise, "If you abide in Me, and My words abide in you, you will ask what you desire, and it shall be done for you" (John 15:7). By abiding in Him and devoting myself to His words, I'm knocking on the door of answered prayer. Herein are the keys to kingdom power and authority—a door on which I knock daily.

Acts to Revelation: The Epistles are *awesome!* Salvation, healing, stories, practical instruction, prophecy, grace, Jesus—they've got it all. Oh, the Bible is a glorious book and I just love to read it!

The pursuit of Christ in His word gets me up in the morning. Time in the word is my source, my sanity. This is where I receive grace for another day. Yes, I *love* daily Bible reading in the secret place!

I find it helpful to read in four different sections of Scripture daily for two main reasons:

1. Momentum. The variety keeps me interested and engaged. Even if my reading in one section doesn't feel inspirational in the moment, my reading in another section may inspire me that day. When I'm interested and engaged, I find the *momentum* to stay with it.

2. Perspective. A point made in one section will sometimes recur in another section. Or a truth in one section will be seen in a totally different light because of a truth in another section. Scripture will start to ricochet off Scripture. When one Scripture gives *perspective* to another Scripture, the Bible will glisten for you with new light. Your heart will come alive with fresh understanding. New vistas of

revelation will expand your heart and ignite your passions. Once this starts to happen for you, you're hooked. Over the edge. Gone.

I hope you're catching this awesome little secret. You'll find momentum and perspective by reading simultaneously in a few different Bible sections each day.

CHAPTER TWENTY-ONE

The Secret of Praying Scripture

The Bible is one massive Prayer Book. Nearly every page contains prayer prompts. As you take time in His word, not only is your meditation sweet but you find yourself spontaneously conversing with God in response to the text. The language of Scripture becomes the language of your prayer life.

Praying with the language of God's word is powerful for several reasons, including:

- His word "is living and powerful" (Hebrews 4:12), so when we pray with His word on our lips, our prayers are living and powerful.
- Praying the word gives us confidence we're praying according to God's will. When we know our request is in His will, *we know that we have the petitions that we have asked of Him* (1 John 5:15).
- As we speak God's word back to Him, our tongue is ignited by the fire of heaven rather than the fire of hell (compare Acts 2:3-4 with James 3:6).
- We're equipped to pray in ways we wouldn't have considered without the text's prompts. The word opens us to new ways of praying, profoundly widening the breadth and diversity of our prayer life.
- Praying the Scriptures adds a dimension of creativity and surprise to our prayer life, which in turn makes prayer more fascinating and enjoyable.

If you've never prayed the Scriptures, I want to get you hooked. Go after this and you'll uncover one of the greatest secrets to making your secret place relationship with Jesus more delightful and fruitful than ever.

First, though, we need a proper definition of prayer. Prayer, in the biblical sense, is the overarching term to describe the entire spectrum of expressions we offer to God. Thus, prayer includes praise, thanksgiving, adoration, intercession, worship, supplication, shouts of joy, lifting of hands, bowing, honor, exaltation, intimate affection, repentance, surrender, dancing, mourning, contemplation, spiritual warfare, prophesying, etc. When the Scriptures form and inform your prayers, you'll start to explore the whole gamut of expressions. Heaven will give you a holy permission slip to do it all!

How do we pray the Scriptures? The best way I know to answer that is to simply do it together. Turn to a portion of Scripture and let's try this thing out. Let me suggest we start with a psalm because the Psalms are all prayers, custom-made for this sort of thing. We could go with any of the 150 Psalms, but I'm going to arbitrarily choose Psalm 84. Turn to Psalm 84, and I'll give you some suggestions for praying it.

Watch for emphatic words in each verse that can be springboards for prayer. Choose a key word or isolate a phrase, and then practice developing that word or concept in prayer. As you explore that concept, ideas from other portions of Scripture may come to mind. No verse is off limits here. You can pull language from any other Scripture as you develop the verse before you. Take anywhere from one to ten minutes with each verse in Psalm 84, praying your way through the psalm one verse at a time. Try it. You'll get a feel for this simply by doing it.

Let me coach you through each verse.

"How lovely is Your tabernacle, O LORD of hosts!" (Psalm 84:1).

- Tell the Lord how many things you find to be *lovely* about Him.

- Your heart is His *tabernacle* of residence; give thanks for the lovely things He's been doing in you.
- The congregation of saints is also His *tabernacle*; praise Him for the *lovely* things He's doing in His people, the church.
- As *Lord of hosts*, He is Captain of heaven's armies. Worship Him! Extol His power.

(As an example, I will "pray" that verse in this paragraph, placing in italics the words in my prayers that are drawn from verse 1: Oh Lord, how *lovely* You are! Wherever You live is *lovely* because You are *lovely*! You make everything that surrounds You *lovely*. Oh, how I long to dwell in Your *habitation*, Lord. I just want to be with You, enjoying You, and being made *lovely* by You. I would rather be with You than anywhere else. The panorama of Your *tabernacle* is altogether marvelous to me, too. I consider the angels, the seraphim, the living creatures, the twenty-four elders, all gathered around Your throne and fixated upon You. Little wonder—You are unsurpassed in beauty and splendor! O *Lord of hosts*, O mighty champion of heaven, O great warrior of glory, I bow before Your majestic greatness today. What an honor to appear before You! Thank you for the blood of Christ that grants me bold access to Your presence. Now that I'm with You, I've arrived at my destination and have nowhere else to go. I worship You, O mighty God!)

"My soul longs, yes, even faints for the courts of the LORD; my heart and my flesh cry out for the living God" (Psalm 84:2).

- Tell Him how you yearn for Him. Let Him see the emotions of your soul at this very moment.
- As you stand at attention before the great King in His courts, express how you're totally available to Him.
- Cry out to God, not just with your heart, but also with your *flesh* (your lungs).

(As another example, here's my prayer just now from verse 2, with italics on the words triggering my prayer: Oh how I *yearn* for You, my God! Every part of my being *longs* for You. I *long* for You with my *soul*, mind, emotions, body, spirit, *heart*, *flesh*, with my everything! I want You more than anything in all creation. If I can just have You, Lord, You're my exceeding great reward. If You don't reveal Yourself to me I'm going to *faint* with *longing*. I'm lovesick for You, *faint* with love. I desire Your *courts* because that's where You live. I just want to be where You live, for all eternity. So here I stand, *crying* out to You, my God. Will You look upon my *cry*? Will You behold my tears? Will you consider the travail of my *soul*? Will You have mercy on me? You are the only God, the true and *living God*, and to You alone my soul rises. Oh, when will You come to me?)

"Even the sparrow has found a home, and the swallow a nest for herself, where she may lay her young—even Your altars, O LORD of hosts, my King and my God" (Psalm 84:3).

- Tell Him how much you want to be with Him, continually—to the point of being envious of a bird that can make its home in the altars of God.
- Tell Him that your heart finds its home in Him.
- Worship your King and God.

(Offer your prayers now to God, in a manner similar to mine in the two previous verses. Express your heart to God, in your own words, based upon the content of verse 3.)

"Blessed are those who dwell in Your house; they will still be praising You. Selah" (Psalm 84:4).

- Thank Him for the perpetual blessing you enjoy because you're continually in His presence.

- Articulate the resolve of your heart to never stop offering sacrifices of praise. It's not just something you do; it's who you are.
- Take some "Selah" moments (time of reflection) to praise Him freely and spontaneously.

"Blessed is the man whose strength is in You, whose heart is set on pilgrimage" (Psalm 84:5).

- Confess your weakness, and your dependence on Him for every ounce of strength.
- Tell Him again that you're a pilgrim, just passing through this land in search of a heavenly city whose maker is God.
- Thank Him for the pathway He's ordained for your pilgrimage. It hasn't always been the path you wanted, but it's been good and wise.

"As they pass through the Valley of Baca, they make it a spring; the rain also covers it with pools" (Psalm 84:6).

- Even though they're rarely enjoyable, thank Him for the valleys of life. Tell Him about your present valley.
- Baca means *Weeping*. Emote to Him from your heart, even to tears.
- Confess your confidence in His leadership, because He's enabling you to turn the darkness of your valley into a place of springs and pools—into a fruitful garden.

"They go from strength to strength; each one appears before God in Zion" (Psalm 84:7).

- The valley may be a place of weakness but thank God He's leading you forward to another pinnacle of strength.

- Rejoice that God is going to turn the darkness of your valley into a face-to-face encounter with Him in His glory.

"O LORD God of hosts, hear my prayer; give ear, O God of Jacob! Selah" (Psalm 84:8).

- Pour out your heart to Him. Tell Him how desperately you long for Him to hear you.
- Worship the God who, even as He was faithful to Jacob, will also be faithful to you. He will defend and save you!
- Recount to the Lord how He defended Jacob, and ask Him for the same blessings.

"O God, behold our shield, and look upon the face of Your anointed" (Psalm 84:9).

- Tell the Lord that He alone is your shield. Ask for protection, security, and help.
- Since you have an anointing from above, beseech God to look upon you with favor and mercy.
- Pray for the anointed leader of your church.

"For a day in Your courts is better than a thousand. I would rather be a doorkeeper in the house of my God than dwell in the tents of wickedness" (Psalm 84:10).

- This is a great verse to help you express how much you love Him. One day in His outer courts is more delightful and exhilarating than a thousand days elsewhere.
- Tell Him your heart isn't set on high and lofty things; you're happy with being just a doorkeeper for Him.
- Call on His mercy, that you might live in His presence forever, and never fall back to the ways of the wicked.

"For the LORD God is a sun and shield; the LORD will give grace and glory; no good thing will He withhold from those who walk uprightly" (Psalm 84:11).

- As your sun, tell Him He's the light of your life, your radiance, your source of warmth, the one who lights your path.
- Worship your shield—the Lord your protector.
- Receive His grace and glory right now.
- Tell Him you believe in His goodness. He'll never withhold it because of your upright walk.
- Tell Him you're determined to walk uprightly in all of life because you love Him so much. Ask for help to always walk uprightly.

"O LORD of hosts, blessed is the man who trusts in You!" (Psalm 84:12).

- Thank Him that this verse describes you!
- Tell Him how much you trust Him.
- Worship the Lord of the warring hosts of heaven, for He's releasing His blessings to you.

As you pray Scripture, don't fear repetition. The repetition of meaningful words and phrases enables truth to lodge more permanently in our hearts. We want the word to pierce us, grab our attention, expand our longing, shape our speech and actions, and bear eternal fruit.

Keep praying the Scriptures until you're hooked! Once you come alive to the secret of praying the word, you'll take your Bible *everywhere*—to your secret place, job, home group, church, and prayer meetings. You'll even find yourself praying the word while driving your car!

What a mighty gift God has given in His word. He's given

us a way to bypass the self-centered, human-based, pity-filled praying we'd normally fall into. Instead, through His word, we share His mind, thoughts, expressions, and priorities. We have a tool to pray His will in the power of the Holy Spirit. Awesome!

CHAPTER TWENTY-TWO

The Secret of Finishing

Sometimes our secret place is interrupted by forces beyond our control. Emergencies happen. And sometimes commitments like work, school, or family require us to pull away.

Occasionally that can leave us feeling like, *I'm not finished yet! Lord, I want more time with You. I'm definitely going to return to this before the day is over. We'll pick up right here where we're leaving off.*

The Lord understands when the demands of life pull us away from the secret place. He's not frowning or displeased. In fact, He loves it when we sincerely wish we could take longer in His presence.

Having made that disclaimer, I want to suggest an element to the secret place that may be an important key for you. It concerns *finishing* your time with Him before moving on to the next thing.

Each visit to the secret place is an event in itself. It often starts with a warm-up period. Sometimes we need a little time before we feel really connected to the Lord at the heart level. But the event doesn't only have a start, it also has a finish. To find a sense of completion of what God intends, sometimes we need to linger until we receive the Lord's release. It can be easy, even unintentionally, to leave before He's done.

Consider this verse about Jesus' prayer life: "Now it came to pass, as He was praying in a certain place, when He ceased, that one of His disciples said to Him, 'Lord, teach us to pray, as John also taught his disciples'" (Luke 11:1). When Jesus' prayer time was complete, He *ceased*. Technically, we know Jesus prayed without ceasing; but as regarded His secret place, a point in time came when He *ceased*. His secret place was finished. In fact, the New American Standard Bible even words it that way: *after He had finished.*

One of the secrets of the secret place is staying with it until you're finished. Discerning when you're done may feel differently each time, according to the Spirit's leading, but I'm suggesting the decision of when to finish is not primarily ours but God's. Let Him decide when it's over. *Give the King the honor of dismissing you.*

Solomon wisely said, "Do not be hasty to go from the king's presence" (Ecclesiastes 8:3). If it's true of earthly kings, how much more for those who draw near to the presence of the King of kings? Having come boldly into His presence through the blood of Christ, we shouldn't be hasty to leave. Slow down, wait on Him, and minister to Him until He gives the release. After all, He knows the demands of our day even better than we.

To uncover the greatest joys of His presence, we must learn to linger. A hit-and-run approach won't take us there. We don't find the potential of intimacy with God on the fly. To find what Jesus had, we want to stay there until it's time to *cease.*

You're welcome to "test drive" this secret. Don't quit till you're finished. Devote yourself to the King until He signals your dismissal and sends you into your world. The intimacy of His chambers will ignite your soul, and you'll carry His fragrance to people who desperately long for what you've found.

CHAPTER TWENTY-THREE

The Secret of the Morning

Don't do it!

Don't skip this chapter. It's tempting to look at this chapter's title and think, *I'm not even going to go there. I'm not a morning person, and I don't want to read about how the morning is the optimum time for the secret place. I've tried it, and it doesn't work for me. I'm a night person and that's my best time.*

That's *great!* If night is your best time, *give God your best.* No one's secret life with Jesus is identical to anyone else's. You're amazingly unique, and the Lord loves the particular spice that arises to Him from your life. Give Him the portion of your day that works best for your personality, frame, and schedule.

For many of us, the morning represents our *best* because our minds are clear and alert. For some, it's our most *valuable* time of day because we're more energetic, creative, and productive. If that's the case, wouldn't that be the perfect time to pray?

For people who work a midnight shift, their *morning* might start around 5:00 p.m. The time on the clock is not the point here. The point is to give Jesus the *best* and *most valuable* time of your day.

I have friends who are night people but prefer the morning for their secret place. One friend told me, *I'm not a morning person, but early morning is the time that produces the greatest rewards for me.*

Another friend said, *I'm not a morning person*, but then she added, *I noticed that when I have my devotions in the morning His word is more fresh to me. So I've started to discipline myself to have my quiet time with God in the morning. I'm more equipped to handle what gets thrown at me in the course of the day.* However, she also added that she uses evening for Bible reading.

I've heard from more than one person that it's helpful to have a set *time* and *place* for meeting with God. It helps build consistency, which in turn produces stronger rewards in our relationship with Christ.

What's the right time of day? Well, God came to visit with Adam and Eve *in the cool of the day* (Genesis 3:8), which would have been either morning or evening. Isaac used the quiet of the evening to talk to God (Genesis 24:63). Daniel prayed morning, mid-day, and evening. Both David and our Lord Jesus modeled an early morning secret life with God.

David wrote, "Early will I seek You" (Psalm 63:1). The word *early* means three things to me:

- I'll seek Him early in life, while I'm young.
- I'll seek Him early in the process, when problems surface, instead of coming to Him after exhausting all my other options.
- I'll seek Him early in the day.

We get a peek into David's prayer life here: "O God, my heart is steadfast; I will sing and give praise, even with my glory. Awake, lute and harp! I will awaken the dawn" (Psalm 108:1-2). David was resolute about the priority of the secret place. When he said his heart was *steadfast*, I think he was steadfast in commitment, and that enabled him to remain steadfast in fervency. He must have known a secret because he was determined to *awaken the dawn*.

Jesus also modeled a pattern of rising early to pray. "Now in the morning, having risen a long while before daylight, He went out and departed to a solitary place; and there He prayed" (Mark 1:35). Interestingly, that particular morning was a Sunday. The day before had been a Sabbath (Saturday), and had been extremely full. He had taught in the synagogue, healed Peter's mother-in-law, visited over dinner, and then at sundown He was thronged by a crowd. Once the Sabbath expired at sundown, Jesus was instantly mobbed. The people swarmed Him for His healing touch. It was suddenly a very busy night.

We're not told how far into the night the meeting went. All we know is that, the next morning, He rose *a long while before daylight* and took off to find a secluded place. Did the intensity of the previous evening's ministry make Him especially eager to be with His Father in the morning? One thing seems clear: It wasn't an especially long night.

Even when His body craved more sleep, Jesus knew revitalization wouldn't come on His back but on His face.

In speaking of Jesus' prayer life, David wrote, "In the beauties of holiness, from the womb of the morning, You have the dew of Your youth." *The womb of the morning.* What a fantastic way to describe Jesus' secret place! The secret place was Jesus' womb of the morning. That's where life incubated, where creativity germinated, where inspiration gestated, where power percolated. When Jesus emerged from this womb of happy holiness, He was revitalized in *the dew of His youth.* The secret place made Him feel vibrant all over again and ready to fulfill the Father's mandate.

Thus, Psalm 110:3 described three aspects of Jesus' secret place relationship with His Father:

- Intimacy: "In the beauties of holiness" indicates proximity of presence.
- Impregnation: "from the womb of the morning" points to life-producing, procreative power.
- Invigoration: "You have the dew of Your youth" speaks of revitalization and renewal of strength.

Jesus experienced intimacy, impartation, and invigoration in His secret life with God, *and you can, too!* Not sure whether to do morning or evening? Experiment with either. Hey—why not do *both*? Give the Alpha and Omega the first and last of your day. He deserves our *best!*

CHAPTER TWENTY-FOUR

The Secret of Getting Dressed

Satan reserves some of his most heated attacks for that moment when we step into the secret place—because he hates what happens when we connect with God. He sees to it that our sins, failures, and shortcomings come to mind and play before our eyes. Some of us even subconsciously avoid the secret place because we don't want to face the barrage of shame and accusation that the enemy hammers us with when we try to pray.

We've been warned that Satan accuses us *before our God day and night* (Revelation 12:10). He doesn't accuse when we're contemplating compromise; he accuses when we decide to come before God. For starters, realize that his accusations are *par for the course.* Every believer experiences this. It's an occupational hazard of the secret place.

Satan's accusations function on at least four levels:

- He accuses God to us. Satan will point to the way God is fathering us and say, *Look at how God is treating me!* (His accusations always sound like your own voice talking to you, but the negative thoughts actually come from him.) *I can't believe God is making me go through all this. They say He's good, but there's nothing good about the way He's treating me. Is He really for me? Can I really trust Him? Will He ever fulfill His promises?* The accuser wants us to get on his side and accuse God with him. When we choose to love God in the midst of our pain, we're actually doing spiritual warfare in a powerful way against Satan's schemes.
- He accuses us to God. He tells God, in our hearing, of our abysmal failures. He paints us as totally unworthy

to draw near. God isn't fazed by Satan's lies—He's been hearing them for centuries—but sometimes we are. Sometimes we suppose God might agree with our accuser. We imagine He's mad at us and doesn't want us near when we're in such a condition.

- He accuses us to each other. He'll tell us that other believers don't accept us. He'll try to cause breaches of relationship in the body of Christ.
- He accuses us to ourselves. This is where he really excels. He's expert at berating us for our sins and weaknesses—especially when we're wanting to get close to the Lord.

What are we to do in the face of such assaults? The Scriptures answer this question clearly because the Lord wants to give us confidence to draw near. Here are some of the ways we overcome the accuser:

- Confess and repent. Satan's accusations carry a sting because they often contain an element of truth. So go ahead, get violent. Confess your sin, call it in its worst terms, repent, and ask forgiveness. *So what* if it's the umpteenth time? I know who I am. I'm not a sinner who struggles to love God; I'm a lover of God who struggles with sin. I'm His child and I love my Father! I come to Him with confidence, confessing any known sin or compromise, and receiving His forgiveness.
- Get under the blood. Ask Jesus to sprinkle you with His blood. The blood of Jesus is our greatest gift! The shed blood of Calvary is so powerful that it actually cleanses us from a defiled conscience (Hebrews 10:22). When the blood of Jesus is over your life, the accuser is speechless. With his accusations silenced, I come boldly to the throne of grace. I'm welcome in the secret place of the Most High because of Christ's shed blood!

> I want to get so under the blood that, when the Father looks at me, all He can see is the blood. I want to get so under the blood that, when Satan looks at me, all he can see is the blood.[1]

- Get dressed. What I mean is, "Put on the Lord Jesus Christ" (Romans 13:14). How do we do that? By putting on the full armor of God. Here's how we do that:

> Put on the whole armor of God, that you may be able to stand against the wiles of the devil. For we do not wrestle against flesh and blood, but against principalities, against powers, against the rulers of the darkness of this age, against spiritual hosts of wickedness in the heavenly places. Therefore take up the whole armor of God, that you may be able to withstand in the evil day, and having done all, to stand. Stand therefore, having girded your waist with truth, having put on the breastplate of righteousness, and having shod your feet with the preparation of the gospel of peace; above all, taking the shield of faith with which you will be able to quench all the fiery darts of the wicked one. And take the helmet of salvation, and the sword of the Spirit, which is the word of God; praying always with all prayer and supplication in the Spirit, being watchful to this end with all perseverance and supplication for all the saints (Ephesians 6:11-18).

Look at each piece of armor.

Getting dressed starts with the *belt of truth*. The truth of God's word is a belt that tightens our waist so we can run. God's truth exposes the lies of Satan's accusations. Believe and speak God's truth about who Christ is in you. Truth gives us confidence to stand before God.

Next, we put on the *breastplate of righteousness*. We've been given the righteousness of God in Christ, and it protects our heart.

With the *shoes of preparation* we prepare ourselves to walk inside enemy lines so we can share the gospel of peace.

The *shield of faith* is a safeguard that no accusation of the

---

1 For more on this, see my book, *Power Of The Blood.*

enemy can penetrate.

The *helmet of salvation* protects our mind from Satan's lies.

The *sword of the Spirit* enables us to engage in offensive warfare against the enemy.

The passage calls us *to stand.* When you step into the secret place, you don't have to go looking for a fight, it will come to you. All you need do is stand. Stand in truth, stand under the blood, and stand before God. When you simply stand before God, the enemy has lost the battle.

When you put on the armor of God, you're actually putting on Christ. Jesus personifies every piece of armor. He's truth, righteousness, peace, faith, salvation, the word. When the Father looks at you, He sees Jesus and welcomes you into His embrace. He not only favors you, He *prefers* you!

Here's the secret: *When we realize we're clothed in the very garments of Christ, our confidence before God soars.* Satan's accusations just bounce off our shield of faith. All the accusations are silenced and we know we're accepted by the Father. We relax, and completely enjoy our secret place visit with Jesus.

Maybe you noticed this already, but when Paul told us to put on the armor of God, he closed the passage by saying, *praying always with all prayer and supplication in the Spirit.* We get dressed *so we can pray.* We get dressed for the secret place.

Hit with accusations? Get dressed!

CHAPTER TWENTY-FIVE

The Secret of Self-Denial

> Then Jesus said to His disciples, "If anyone desires to come after Me, let him deny himself, and take up his cross, and follow Me" (Matthew 16:24).

Jesus invited us to share in His cross. Someone might suppose Jesus saying, *Since I have to suffer so much to procure your salvation, I want you to suffer, too.* But Jesus wasn't intending a morbid invitation to pain; He was giving a glorious invitation to intimacy with Him.

If you really want to be close to Me, He's telling us, *then let Me give you the key. Deny yourself, take up your cross, and follow Me.* It's an invitation to deep camaraderie, but we often avoid the cross because we're repulsed by the idea of suffering. But have we understood what we're buying? It's like someone offering us a brand-new Mercedes sedan for $20, and us bemoaning the fact that they're trying to extract $20 from us. Next to what we're buying, the cost is *nothing*! Yes, self-denial comes at a price, but it's nothing in comparison to the privilege of walking in intimate communion with the King.

If you can receive it, here's the secret: *Self-denial can help propel you forward into greater joys of intimacy.* Self-denial and intimacy have kissed. Self-denial unshackles and liberates the flow of love in the secret place.

Denying oneself is not the same as taking up one's cross. Taking up the cross has to do, in part, with crucifying *sinful* desires. Self-denial, on the other hand, regards *good, healthy* desires. Self-denial is the deliberate curtailing of healthy appetites for the sake of increasing the pace of our pursuit. We want to keep up with Jesus.

What are some of the ways self-denial might be expressed?

- Fasting from food, drink, media
- Cutting back on sleep time
- Bypassing good entertainment
- Declining attractive social invitations
- Reducing recreation time
- Taking a short-term vow of celibacy
- Spending less when you can afford more
- Etc.

None of these activities being denied are sinful. Practiced in moderation and wisdom, they're gifts of God that we might enjoy a fulfilling and satisfying life. But some people want more than a happy life; they want to know Jesus. They're reaching for kingdom conquest, desiring eternal treasure, and longing for the Spirit's outpouring, Self-denial is a gift that enables them to intensify the furnace of their love.

Let's look at some of self-denial's benefits.

Clearer perspective

When you deny yourself, scales fall from your eyes. The more you deny yourself, the more you'll see. You'll begin to see the world for what it is (we naturally get desensitized to the filth of the world system that surrounds us). The world denies itself nothing, so when you embrace self-denial you're doing something other-worldly. We deny ourselves because we don't love the world or the things in the world.

Remember how the prodigal son came to his senses? From lack of food: "But when he came to himself, he said, 'How many of my father's hired servants have bread enough and to spare, and I perish with hunger!'" (Luke 15:17). He had to starve in order to see. Voluntary fasting has a similar way of helping us regain spiritual focus. A good fast will give you a spiritual chiropractic adjustment.

Accelerated change

When the scales fall from your eyes because of self-denial, you'll see how worldliness has seeped into your lifestyle. As you respond in contrite humility, Jesus will release grace for change. He always gives grace to the humble (1 Peter 5:5). He'll show you things you had no idea needed to change. The accelerated change that comes from self-denial is a beautiful thing.

Fasting prepares us for change. In speaking of fasting, Jesus said, *New wine must be put into new wineskins* (Mark 2:22). He meant that fasting refurbishes the crusty, old wineskins of our hearts and makes them new again. It prepares us for new wine. Fasting is a powerful element in preparing us for the new wine of God's fresh movements today.

Preparation for prophetic ministry

Is God calling you to speak prophetically to something excessive in our culture? Then you'll need to practice self-denial. When something is practiced in excess, you can't have a voice to it while practicing it in moderation. To have a voice to the excessive, you must sanctify yourself from even the moderate, balanced expression of that practice.

Jesus modeled this principle. To address the greed of the Pharisees, He wouldn't even allow His hands to touch money. To address their attachment to possessions, He didn't allow Himself even a place to lay His head. Jesus sanctified Himself from the good and normal in order to have a voice into the excessive and imbalanced.

Those who carry a prophetic message to the body of Christ will sometimes embrace an uncommon self-denial. Like John the Baptist, self-denial can lend authority to a messenger's message.

Ability to hear God

We've said that self-denial helps us *see* better, but I want to add that it also helps us *hear* better. When I need to hear from God, I'll typically go on a fast. Answers, guidance, direction, insight—all seem to flow more freely in context to grace-empowered self-denial.

Mike Bickle calls fasting *voluntary weakness*. It makes us weaker in our bodies. We don't usually like to be weak, but in self-denial we willingly weaken ourselves so we might access greater grace. Those who embrace voluntary weakness place their confidence in these words of Jesus: "My grace is sufficient for you, for My strength is made perfect in weakness" (2 Corinthians 12:9). We may be weaker in our bodies but we're stronger in our spirits—stronger to hear the Lord's voice.

Jesus connected the secret place with self-denial. He said,

> "Moreover, when you fast, do not be like the hypocrites, with a sad countenance. For they disfigure their faces that they may appear to men to be fasting. Assuredly, I say to you, they have their reward. But you, when you fast, anoint your head and wash your face, so that you do not appear to men to be fasting, but to your Father who is in the secret place; and your Father who sees in secret will reward you openly" (Matthew 6:16-18).

Self-denial is practiced in secret. We intentionally avoid being seen by men, but reserve our consecration for His eyes only. Fasting can be a very affectionate element in your secret relationship with Him.

Want in on a secret? When your secret place needs revitalization, embrace the grace of self-denial. Throw in some fasting. Your heart will be more vulnerable to the impressions of the Spirit, you'll soar higher in love, and your awareness of His presence will increase.

CHAPTER TWENTY-SIX

The Secret of Boredom

Ever get bored while praying?

Let's be real: *Everyone* does. The myth that your quiet time with Jesus is going to be invigorating every day is just that—a myth. I'm dropping another little secret right here: Everybody gets bored in their secret place. Cat's out of the bag. And you thought you were the only one, ha. Even the *twelve apostles of the Lamb* fell asleep during a prayer meeting presided by Jesus Himself (Matthew 26:40-45)!

Some days you'll enjoy a really good connection with God, and you'll be like, *Why isn't it like this all the time?* But in reality, there are a lot of deadpan days mixed in with the great ones.

Sometimes it's because I'm tired and bleary. Other times, I'm awake enough, but there seems to be no movement of the Spirit on my heart. On some days, it doesn't seem to matter what passage I read or how fervently I pray, it's just going to be dull.

And I'm not alone. This is our common experience because we're weak human beings who struggle to find the kind of connection with God we desire. Jesus was speaking about our brokenness in prayer when He said, "The spirit indeed is willing, but the flesh is weak" (Matthew 26:41).

What should we do, then, when we're bored? Do it anyway. Persevere. Do the time. Grind it out. Bite the bullet.

Allow nothing to dissuade or discourage you, boredom included. Somewhere along the way, we need to cement a life decision: "I'm devoting myself by God's grace to the secret place, come rain or shine, good days or bad, when I feel like it or when I don't, when it's easy and when it's hard." Make that resolve and I promise, the grace of Christ *will* enable you.

Call out for help! Jesus gave us the Holy Spirit to be our *Helper* in times of need (John 14:16). Call on your Helper. *Holy Spirit, I need You right now. I don't know how to do this. Help!* You'll be amazed at the things that change inside when you cry, "Holy Spirit, help." He *loves* to help us pray! But He wants to be invited.

Paul told how the Holy Spirit empowers our prayer lives: "Likewise the Spirit also helps in our weaknesses. For we do not know what we should pray for as we ought, but the Spirit Himself makes intercession for us with groanings which cannot be uttered" (Romans 8:26). To go deeper in prayer, explore the Holy Spirit's partnership in your prayer life.

When I fall asleep in the secret place, I don't allow the enemy to use that against me. I just see myself as His little child, curled up and restful in His arms. I believe He smiles on me just for showing up. I could have fallen asleep elsewhere, but I chose to do it in His embrace.

I want to expose the enemy's schemes right now. He tries to use our inadequacies to shame us away from meeting with God. He does this with all of us. He wants us to believe that, while everyone else has a great secret place, we're a unique oddball who is never going to have an effective prayer life. It's not true. You're experiencing the same prayer territory *all* the saints of history have traversed. The apostles and prophets? Even *they* knew what it was like for prayer to be lifeless and the Scriptures to chew like sawdust.

Your struggle is common to all of us.

But let me remind you of what we said earlier in this book. If you'll keep sowing to the secret place, even in boring times, you will eventually reap. One day of exhilaration in the Holy Spirit is worth a thousand days of sowing! (Psalm 84:10) It's really true. Once God touches you with His Spirit and energizes you with His word, you're hooked for life. You don't care how long the wilderness might last, you're going to keep walking because you know on the other side is an oasis of heavenly encounter.

Okay, here comes another secret. The more seasoned and experienced you become in the secret place, *the dull days get fewer*. It keeps getting better. Just stick with it! Your momentum is only going to grow.

Here's my point: Don't be thrown off by boredom. Take it in stride and press through. You'll be so glad you stayed with it.

The most valuable things in the kingdom of God always come at the steepest price (Revelation 3:18). Boredom? Small price to pay!

CHAPTER TWENTY-SEVEN

The Secret of Feeling Attractive to God

When you come before God, how do you think He looks at you? Your answer is critical to the success of your secret life. If you're confident in His acceptance, you'll come to the secret place eagerly and frequently. The accuser knows this, so he'll cast your Father as disapproving. Satan wants you to see your Father as harsh, demanding, disappointed, never satisfied with what you do, and frustrated with your spiritual growth.

If that caricature of your heavenly Father resembles the image you carry on the inside, it will negatively affect how you relate to Him. You'll be disconnected emotionally, hesitant to draw near, and weary of trying to please Him. You'll be robbed of the joy of loving Him freely.

Nothing is deadlier to the secret place than a false idea of how God views you; and nothing is more empowering than when your mind is renewed to understand how He looks on you. When you gain ownership of the truth that He's smiling on you and longing to be close, your emotional chemistry changes. You actually begin to *feel* attractive to God. This changes everything about how you relate to Him.

It starts with understanding how God feels about the cross of Christ. The cross stands before Him as a constant, blazing, unforgettable memorial. It's as fresh in His mind today as the day it happened. We know this because, in Revelation 5:6, Jesus is standing before the throne as a Lamb *as though it had been slain*. To God, it's as though Jesus was slain just moments ago. Two thousand years hasn't erased from God's heart one iota of the horror and power of Calvary. Just mention the cross and you're the touching eternal passions of an uncreated God.

When you place your faith in that cross, you move God in His deepest places. He opens the storehouses of His heart and lavishes you with acceptance, affirmation, and exuberant delight. All you have to do is believe in the cross and you're *in!* You're His child.

You're not just family, you're *good-looking* family. You now carry the family resemblance, and the Father thinks you're stunningly delightful.

When you know you're attractive to God, you come into His presence with boldness. And that's exactly how He wants you to come! He wants you approaching Him with lifted face, expectant eyes, a big smile, an eager voice, and a confident heart.

He doesn't enjoy you any less because you struggle. He knows how weak you are because He made you. He enjoys you even when you fall. When you blow it, He urges you to pick yourself up and start walking again toward Him. We present ourselves to Him with all our shortcomings and let Him see everything because we know He delights greatly in us. He enjoys every phase of our development.

Psalm 45:11 reveals how Jesus feels when He looks at you: "So the King will greatly desire your beauty." *You are stunningly beautiful to Jesus!* In Psalm 45, Jesus is a Bridegroom King and you're His bride. He looks upon you with desire. He wants to have and hold you. When you come to the secret place, you're coming into His chambers. It's a place of beauty, longing, intimacy, and delight. He longs for you!

Maybe we could call this *the secret of appeal*. He finds us appealing and attractive. When we know this, we want to return to His chambers frequently.

As we spend time in His glory, we're changed even *more* into His image (2 Corinthians 3:18). And that in turn means that we become—if it were possible—even *more* attractive to Him! *The hidden person of the heart* (1 Peter 3:3) is made increasingly beautiful in the hidden place of the Most High.

He'll awaken in you the bridal cry of Song of Solomon 8:6, "Set me as a seal upon your heart." This is the bride saying to her Beloved, "Let Your life be bound up in mine. Fasten all Your affections on me. Make me the center of Your universe. I don't want You to *feel* anything without including me, and I don't want You to *do* anything without including me. Make your passions mine. Make Your thoughts my thoughts. I want to be joined to You in love. Forever."

It's a cry to become His soul mate. A soul mate is someone who not only arrives at the same conclusions as you, but they get there the same way. They think like you. They respond to circumstances like you. If you ask, Jesus will change you and make you into His soul mate. He'll set you as a seal on His heart—in the secret place.

He calls you *the apple of His eye* (Deuteronomy 32:10; Zechariah 2:8), You're the most precious thing He looks upon. He values and protects you in the same way we guard the pupil of our eye.

The Scriptures say that Jacob's life was *bound up* in the life of his son, Benjamin (Genesis 44:30), meaning that Benjamin meant the *world* to him. In the same way, your Father's life is *bound up* in yours. He lives when you live. He thrills when you're fulfilled. He rejoices when you're liberated. He's content when you're at rest. You're the center of His universe.

Jesus testified that the Father loves us *just as He loves Jesus* (John 17:23). Think of it! God feels the same way about us as He feels about His holy, spotless, selfless Son. We're as attractive to the Father as Jesus. Incredible!!

God feels much more strongly about me than I do about Him. Even when my zeal for Him is hot and bright, it doesn't approach the intensity of His love for me. Here's one way I've noticed this to be true. I can think about only one thing at a time so, when I go to work, sometimes God will be absent from my thoughts for minutes or hours at a time. When my mind returns to the Lord, He's right there. Even while I wasn't thinking of Him, He was thinking of me. And waiting. Waiting for our minds to connect again. He never stops thinking about me (Psalm 139:17). His eyes are riveted and His mind is focused on me—incessantly. I'm just that beautiful to Him.

He *waits* for you to come to Him. He waits all night, watching over your bed, and waiting for you to rise. He's hoping He might be your first thought in your morning. You don't have to wonder if He wants you to come into the secret place. He's been waiting, and He'll continue to wait for as long as necessary—because His heart is bound up in your life.

May you have grace to fully believe this powerful secret: God finds you attractive.

Lord, may I never again withhold myself from Your embrace!

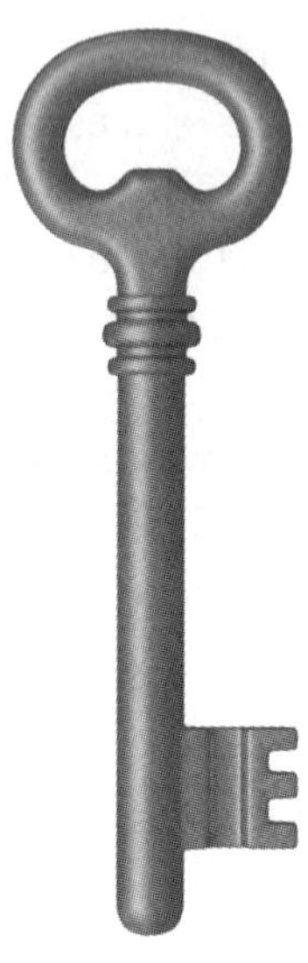

PART III

Setting a Marathon Pace

In this section, let's look at some themes and principles that will position us for the years. We're preparing our hearts to make a lifetime commitment to the secret place. We don't want merely a burst of fresh energy, only to have it dissipate in a few weeks. We want grace-empowered grit to pursue God in the secret place every single day of our lives until we're called home.

CHAPTER TWENTY-EIGHT

The Secret of Desperation

For years I was very disciplined in my devotional life, determined to spend time daily in the word and prayer. I would read through the Bible in a different translation every year. I would sing, worship the Lord, and pray through a long list of people. However, there were heights in the secret place I never discovered until the Lord took me on an unforeseen journey.

He allowed a traumatic calamity to hit my life. Life careened out of control, and my very survival (spiritually) was at stake. Frantically, I began to claw and shove my way into God's heart, scouring Scripture cover to cover to understand His ways. I was like a drowning man fighting for air. Simply put, I was desperate. As I chased after God, the secret place blossomed for me like a desert flower. Why did the desert do it? *Desperation*. It was a critical ingredient I needed to awaken me to the secret place.

Desperation will turn you into another person. A drowning man has only one thought on his mind—*air*. Nothing else matters. Life is reduced to one consuming necessity, to one life-dominating prayer.

The hemorrhaging woman of Mark 5:25 was desperate. She was willing to take crazy chances at being recognized as she pushed her way through the crowd because the only thing she cared about was touching Jesus.

Desperation produces tunnel vision. This is seen in the story of the siege of Samaria. Syria laid siege to the city of Samaria, and the Israelites inside the city were starving—to the point of eating their children. In answer to Elisha's prayer, God terrified the Syrian army so severely that they fled wildly for their lives, leaving behind an unguarded camp with all its provender. When the Israelites realized it was safe to plunder the supplies left in the abandoned camp, all they could see—in their desperation—was *food.* A stampede ensued as the people rushed toward the food supply. The officer who tried to manage the pandemonium was trampled to death at the city's gate (see 2 Kings 6-7). His story illustrates that when people are desperate, you'd better get out of their way or they'll walk over you.

When you're made desperate for God, your pursuit takes on a different tone. Survival is at stake. You get a look in your eye that's almost half-crazed. You'll go anywhere or do anything. No measure is too extreme. You look at other people and think, *I love you, I respect you, I think you're a wonderful person—but if you don't get out of my way I'm going to run you over. Because I have got to touch Jesus!*

Shallow sources of entertainment get tossed. Invitations to parties are spurned. Others start to lose interest in your friendship because they realize you're not much fun anymore. But you don't care—you're desperate for God. All that matters is touching Jesus' garment.

When you seek God with this kind of focus, you trigger a spiritual windstorm. Changes tumble both in you and around you. Angelic activity (both good and evil) increases in intensity around your life, even though you may not be aware of it. You gain the attention of heaven and hell. Issues that simmered for years suddenly come to a head, demanding resolve. You find yourself surrounded by suspicion and reproach. God has you in His accelerated course, and the speed of change and transition surrounding you is dizzying.

And on the inside? You're coming alive to God. His word feeds and sustains you. New insights electrify and carry you. The closeness of His presence intoxicates you. The revelation of His love redefines your relationship with Him. The understanding of His heart and purposes gives you new perspective on the kingdom of God. You're getting addicted to the glories of the secret place!

Someone might be wondering, "Lord, how do I touch what Bob is talking about here?" I can only speak from personal experience. There was nothing I could do to touch this desperation. I needed God's intervention. I needed Him to make me desperate. I called on Him, and He answered me. It had to start on God's end. "For it is God who works in you both to will and to do for His good pleasure" (Philippians 2:13).

I invite you to pray. *Lord, make me desperate for You*. Cry with tears, and He'll hear you. He knows where you're at, He knows what you can bear, and He has an answer. He knows how to make us thirsty for Him.

There *is* a dangerous prayer to pray. Want to know what it is? Okay, I'll tell you. *Whatever it takes*. There, that's it. *Whatever it takes to know You, touch You, be more like You*. It's a dangerous prayer because, if God chooses to answer, everything will change. This is what launched my journey. I believe in praying dangerous prayers!

Don't fear how God might answer. *Perfect love casts out fear* (1 John 4:18). Perfected love knows that anything coming from His hand is good and helps move us toward a hopeful future (Jeremiah 29:11). Perfect love fears nothing God might use to lead us into greater abandonment. Throw wide your arms and embrace His good, acceptable, and perfect will.

God makes us desperate through trouble or struggle. Our first response is to cry for deliverance, but immediate relief would undermine the process. He'll use our distress to produce desperation, and then He'll take us on a journey into things we've longed to touch but didn't know how to get there.

A personal friend, Cindy, suffered for years with chronic pain. The Lord healed her wonderfully and now she ministers, in gratefulness, to others who live with chronic pain. Processing her journey with me, she confided about her secret place relationship with God.

Before her healing, she depended on every word from God to sustain her. She needed hope, strength, and assurances from Him just to keep going. She was needy and realized that He alone was her answer. In a word, she was desperate.

Then, when He answered her prayer and healed her, things changed. She lost that sense of desperation. She felt like she wasn't so dependent on Him anymore. She knew what her secret place was like in her times of desperation, and now it was different. She called it *less intense*.

In a similar vein, I've read stories of believers in China who were imprisoned for their faith and who, after their release, wept for the kind of intimacy with God they had in prison. He was so close in their suffering! Freedom changed that. Some said they missed the former intimacy so much they actually wanted to return to prison.

The silver lining in the dark clouds of hardship is that we become desperate, and desperation drives into the Savior.

None of us wants hardship, and I don't believe we should ask for it. But I do believe in dangerous prayers, such as, *Lord, whatever it takes, I've got to touch the fullness of Your glory and power.* If He receives your cry, He may take you on a spiritual journey of desperation for more of Him.

Don't despise the means God uses to make you desperate for Him. There are realms of intimacy with Jesus, in the secret place, that are found only through holy desperation.

CHAPTER TWENTY-NINE

The Secret of Manna Gathering

When you're desperate for God, you become dependent upon the sustaining power of His word. Feeding on God's word is your source of survival. You need to eat every day, just as the Israelites in the wilderness survived by gathering manna every morning. Their manna was good for only one day; if kept over to the next, it would rot (Exodus 16:12-31). That's because God wanted to illustrate this principle: Yesterday's manna won't sustain us today. We return to the secret place every morning because that's where we gather our daily portion of fresh manna.

Proverbs 16:26 says, "The person who labors, labors for himself, for his hungry mouth drives him on." Spiritual hunger drives us into the secret place. When you feed on God's word you get healthy, and healthy sheep have a voracious appetite for more. Spiritual appetite will drive you into the secret place.

An appetite is a good sign of health, and loss of appetite is alarming. If you lose your hunger for God's word, take it as a danger signal. Your spirit is telling you that something's wrong. It's time for self-examination. Is a cancerous sin destroying your spiritual health? What's wrong, and what must you do to get better?

Just as natural remedies renew our physical person, there are ways to renew our spiritual person. For starters, drink lots of water (be filled with the Spirit). Get sufficient rest (ceasing from your own works). Get plenty of exercise (in the word and prayer). Avoid junk foods (don't replace God's word with substitutes that don't nourish your spirit). If we're careful and self-disciplined, our spiritual appetite can be restored. Never settle for anything less than a hefty appetite for God's word.

Learn how to collect manna for yourself. Christians who rely on a weekly sermon to feed themselves are probably malnourished. Jesus didn't die for us to live off one meal a week. He died to give us an abundant source of life in His word and Spirit. He doesn't want you living off the secret life of your pastor; He wants you to find your own source of life in the secret place. Become a self-feeder.

Once you learn to feed yourself in the word, you no longer depend on a Sunday sermon as your source of nourishment. That's why you're not upset when the worship or preaching in a church service doesn't connect for you. You've got a source in God that goes beyond Sunday morning services (as necessary as they are). You're not looking for others to serve you milk because now you're cutting your own meat.

Some believers have misplaced expectations of what Sunday morning church is about. Yes, it's a place for their kids to be taught and strengthened. And yes, it's a place to be filled with the Spirit and taught in the word. But it's not a replacement for the secret place. Nor is it a replacement for family altar, where parents sit daily with their children, pray with them, and instruct them in the word according to the commandment (Deuteronomy 11:19). When we have unrealistic expectations of Sunday church, we can easily become critical or cynical toward the body of Christ (a disease which can be terminal and is highly infectious, especially with our children).

It's not that difficult to learn how to gather manna. Just get out there and start working. You're going to learn by doing it. Open your Bible and begin to labor in it. At first, you may feel clumsy, but stay with it. The more you labor in the word, the more skilled you'll become at satisfying your spiritual appetite.

As you persevere, you'll discover your secret place will satisfy you in at least three ways:

Feeding in the word

Of the godly it's said, "But his delight is in the law of the LORD, and in His law he meditates day and night. He shall be like a tree planted by the rivers of water, that brings forth its fruit in its season, whose leaf also shall not wither; and whatever he does shall prosper" (Psalm 1:2-3). As the nutrients of God's word feed us, we develop into fruit-bearing trees. Here's the thing about a good fruit tree: It feeds many people. Your life will become a blessing to others.

Drinking in the Spirit

Jesus said, "But whoever drinks of the water that I shall give him will never thirst. But the water that I shall give him will become in him a fountain of water springing up into everlasting life" (John 4:14). The Holy Spirit is water to your spirit. He'll help you swallow the manna of the word. The word nourishes us best when accompanied by generous drafts of the Holy Spirit.

Cultivating a knowing relationship with God

Hebrews 8:11 quotes the Old Testament, "None of them shall teach his neighbor, and none his brother, saying, 'Know the LORD,' for all shall know Me, from the least of them to the greatest of them." God wants to lead you into a hidden place in Him where you develop your own unique connection to Him. He wants your relationship to be like no one else's. Together, you and He will build your own secret history in which you hang together and get to know one another better. Your relationship with Him will be so unique that no person can teach you how to find it. The Holy Spirit Himself will be your teacher. Just shut your door.

When our secret place is vibrant and we're leading our children in understanding God's word, now weekly corporate gatherings can fulfill their proper role in our lives. Church can be a place where God is glorified and ministered to; where a statement is made in the community; where dark principalities are resisted; where we can encourage and support one another; where a godly vision is articulated to the collective body; where unity is built; where corporate prayer ascends to God; where the young and the weak are strengthened; where seekers come to Christ.

Just one more thought. When I was a young pastor, I was always scouring the word for sermon material. I wanted to be faithful before the Lord to feed the flock. But then He arrested me and changed how I relate to the word. Now, I read the Bible just for me. I'm the hungry one, the desperate one, the needy one. I need fresh manna every day just to survive.

And here's what I've found: When Jesus keeps me alive with the words of His mouth, and then I share that manna with others, it feeds them as well. In fact, I've discovered that others are fed more substantially when I simply share with them the things that have first sustained me.

The secret is: Learn to gather your own manna. Then you'll have something to share.

CHAPTER THIRTY

The Secret of Enduring

The Christian race is a marathon not a sprint. To finish the race requires *endurance.* The first place to exercise endurance is the secret place.

All of us know what it's like to go through desert seasons in which the secret place feels dry and dusty. We get through because we made a decision, ever before the dry time hit, that we're going to keep pursuing God no matter how tough the slogging gets. I'll let you in on a secret: A tenacious determination to endure in prayer opens to the most meaningful dimensions of relationship with the Lord.

Most assuredly, the resolve of every runner to endure in prayer is going to be tested by dry seasons.

Seasons are necessary to successful discipleship. We don't do well in unbroken sunshine. A life of constant happiness without any rain clouds produces drought. Nonstop sunshine only creates a desert. We don't enjoy storms but they're essential to the journey and they signal the normal change of seasons.

Endure in good times? Easy. It's when tough times hit that our endurance is proven. When we're hurting, will we endure in prayer?

Jesus showed us what to do when we're hurting. When He was in His greatest distress, He found His garden of prayer—Gethsemane. It says, *And being in agony, He prayed more earnestly* (Luke 22:44). When He hurt He prayed. And when He *really* hurt, He *really* prayed. This was Jesus' secret to completing the greatest race of all time. He did the cross to the finish because He first endured in prayer.

Are you suffering? Pain pushes us either away from or toward God. If we'll harness the pain properly, it can actually be a gift that drives us into the Lord's presence. The more you hurt the more you pray.

Paul prayed the Colossian believers would be strengthened with the power of Christ *for all patience and longsuffering with joy* (Colossians 1:11). When you're in a difficult season that is forcing you to exert *patience and longsuffering*, it's challenging to do so with *joy*. How do you suffer a long time and keep your joy? Certainly not through human strength! This requires the might of heaven—the power of Christ.

Nobody is more experienced in *patience and longsuffering with joy* than God Himself. Consider how much God suffers as He shares the grief of the world. He's been doing it for millennia! But even though His suffering is deeper than any of us comprehend, He's also filled with great joy. Suffering with joy is God-territory, and He has the grace to enable us to do it with Him.

To endure with joy, we need help. That's why we retreat to the solace of the secret place. Here we're strengthened with God's might so we can suffer a long time with joy. Simply put, godly endurance is impossible apart from a sustained secret life with God.

Besides Paul, James also wrote of being joyful in the midst of hardship: "My brethren, count it all joy when you fall into various trials, *knowing* that the testing of your faith produces patience" (James 1:2-3). James emphasized that God has purpose in trials, and when we *know* His purpose we can endure with joy. To understand purpose, we run to the secret place. The secret pursuit of God in His word reveals His purposes in trials. When we read how He carried Bible saints through their hardships, we realize the same grace is extended to carry us to similar victories.

My source of endurance is the Scriptures. Paul spoke of *the patience of the Scriptures* (Romans 15:4) because they're a repository for endurance. Every time I return to them, I'm strengthened in resolve to wait on God alone. They show, over and over, how God reveals His salvation to those who endure.

The purpose of God in trials is illustrated through the metaphor of *pearl*. When an oyster gets an irritant lodged inside its shell, it forms a protective coating over it and creates a pearl. What started as an irritant ended in a valuable treasure. That illustrates how God redeems our sufferings. Initially we're distressed, but in the end we emerge with the pearl of Christlikeness formed within.

The longer the irritant resides inside the oyster's shell, the larger and more valuable the pearl becomes. Therefore, the formative value of tribulation is sometimes directly proportional to the duration of the crucible. The longer the distress, the more valuable the pearl. When we know this, we can endure with joy. There's no other entrance to the eternal city but the *pearly* gates of *treasure perfected in hardship*.

The apostle John provided an example of what can happen when we endure in prayer through hardship. In his old age, he was exiled to the Roman prison island of Patmos. Maybe he lived in a cave or built himself a hut. Being a prisoner in his 90's was grueling. He was infirm, hungry, lonely, and tired. To all appearances, he was ending his days in pointless futility. But in spite of the hardship, being devoted to prayer, *he was in the Spirit on the Lord's Day* (Revelation 1:10).

How did Jesus honor His friend's prayerful endurance? He visited Him in blazing glory and downloaded to him the book of Revelation. Caesar thought he had banished John to a place where his witness would finally be muted, but instead, he was handed a megaphone. John's quill has roared through every century of human history. Enduring prayer turned lockdown into liberty for millions.

When you endure in prayer, Christ's purpose in your life is unstoppable!

Never give up. Get in the Spirit every day. This may be the day that Jesus visits you and changes everything.

CHAPTER THIRTY-ONE

The Secret of Confinement

Like John the prisoner, you may find yourself in a place of restriction, and may be feeling the emotions that accompany imprisonment and confinement. Feelings such as hopelessness, uselessness, despair, abandonment, rejection, reproach, perplexity, loneliness, vulnerability, boredom, etc. With such a host of emotions assaulting the prisoner's equilibrium, it's challenging to maintain an unswerving confidence in the simple secret of this chapter: *When you're confined, God is closer than you realize.*

The Lord assures the afflicted soul, "I will be with him in trouble" (Psalm 91:15). When you're troubled by circumstances that twist and squeeze your soul, that's when the Lord draws especially close and stands with you.

David said of the Lord, *He made darkness His secret place* (Psalm 18:11). When the lights go out and you're plunged into emotional darkness, you're actually being invited into God's secret place. He meets with His beloved elect in the darkest places of life.

The Lord's prison is generally characterized by social isolation and loneliness. Friends drift away, and relationships that were once strong and meaningful become distant or estranged. Your ability to function is curtailed, and you find no joy in the small amount of movement your chains allow. Even though you may feel abandoned, however, this confinement has been orchestrated by your Lover. Your heavenly Husband has allured you into the wilderness (Hosea 2:14). He will comfort you with His presence and renew your delight in His goodness.

Initially, you won't understand why He's brought you into this lonely, aimless wilderness. Perplexity makes us desperate to understand. He'll use the perplexity to motivate you to seek Him with wholehearted abandonment. And that's what He wanted all along—that you run hard after Him. He had to allure you into the wilderness to unlock such eager love. He intends to use the loneliest time of your life to ignite a depth of intimacy you've never known before.

Before, you were too busy to find it. Before, other fountains had nurtured your soul. But now, in the quietness of your cell, He dries up every other fountain that has nurtured your soul. When He becomes the only fountain of your soul, you'll whisper through your tears, *All my springs are in You* (Psalm 87:7).

You used to be energized by projects; now you're energized by a Person.

David spoke of the intimacy of the prison: "You have hedged me behind and before, and laid Your hand upon me. Such knowledge is too wonderful for me; it is high, I cannot attain it" (Psalm 139:5-6). David was *hedged behind*—he couldn't quit because he was being carried forward. He was *hedged before*—he couldn't push ahead any faster than the pace set for him. God's hand was *laid on him*—he couldn't make an escape to the left or the right. He was a man without options. And yet, instead of complaining about the constraints, he viewed such closeness to God as lofty and wonderful.

Another image for this kind of closeness is found with the Shulamite in the Song of Solomon. She said it this way: *His left hand is under my head, and his right hand embraces me* (Song of Solomon 8:3). She viewed the confinement as His loving embrace.

Confinement positions us for an awakening.

Prison isn't just about deepened intimacy; it's also about increased revelation. Jesus said, *Whatever I tell you in the dark, speak in the light* (Matthew 10:27). In a dark prison, you may be distracted because you can't see anything; but then you'll realize, He turned out the lights so He could speak to you. In times of darkness, you may hear God like never before. He may not talk about what *you* want, but He'll talk about the things on *His* heart. If you'll listen in the darkness, you'll have something to say to your generation when the lights come back on.

Are you in a prison of sorts? Just love Him. Solomon said, *A friend loves at all times* (Proverbs 17:17). Even when they don't understand His mysterious ways, His friends still love Him. They love Him through *anything*. In the quietness of your prison, your friendship with Jesus will grow. You'll agree that *faithful are the wounds of a friend* (Proverbs 27:6). Your Friend loved you enough to wound you, so He could woo you into an abiding relationship with Him.

Here's one of the secrets of darkness: *He imprisons those He loves in order to awaken and mature their affections for Him.* Your wilderness is a secret place. Don't despise your chains—they're binding you to the heart of the One you love.

Never waste a good prison sentence. Use the confinement to go deeper in God.

CHAPTER THIRTY-TWO

The Secret of Waiting

The secret place is a time machine, transporting us from our time zone to His. We step into the eternal and view life from the vantage of the Ageless One who is without beginning or ending of days. From here, waiting on God takes on an entirely different hue.

The closer you get to God, the more you realize He's in no hurry. There's no panic in heaven, only calculated purpose. Consequently, we don't act hastily, either (Isaiah 28:16). People of faith don't allow the urgent to press them into frantic action. Faith waits on God until the moment for action is right.

Lord, help me to write about the powerful secret of waiting on You!

When it comes to secret place activities, many of us have these items on our list:

- ✓ Confession of sins
- ✓ Worship, praise, thanksgiving
- ✓ Bible Reading
- ✓ Meditation
- ✓ Intercession
- ✓ Journaling

When those are completed, we suppose our secret place time is done. But think about adding yet one more element to your routine: waiting on God.

Wait on God in the manner depicted in Psalm 123:2, "Behold, as the eyes of servants look to the hand of their masters, as the eyes of a maid to the hand of her mistress, so our eyes look to the LORD our God, until He has mercy on us."

To wait on God is to stare at His hand. Why stare at His hand? Two reasons: We watch for a signal regarding anything He wants done; and we watch for His mighty hand to move on our behalf.

Some people suppose waiting on God is sitting by the pool sipping on lemonade. Actually, it's one of the most violent things you'll ever do. When everything is screaming at you to do something, you're obeying His call to wait on Him alone. You're giving Him your full gaze until He releases mercy.

While waiting *for* God, wait *on* God.

We wait for God to move in power. Someone once said, *We should seek His face and not His hand.* I disagree. We seek His face *and* His hand. We seek the intimacy of His face, but we also seek the power of His hand. We don't have to choose between intimacy and power, we can pursue both. We minister to Him in love *until* He moves on our behalf.

Waiting on God is one of the most difficult spiritual disciplines because many of us aren't accustomed to just sitting and gazing. We want everything to be efficient—even our secret place. But prayer is sometimes wasteful.

Our generation is so easily bored. We lack the attention span to wait on God. But He knows that, so He kindly designs scenarios in which we have no other choice but to wait on Him. He'll graciously help us cross the boredom threshold. Then, waiting on God becomes an adventure—an open field for free roaming.

Waiting on God gets easier when we gain more fulfillment just by being with Him than by working for Him. When being with Him is a satisfying end in itself, we can wait for as long as it takes—just as long as we're with Him. The reason Jesus could wait thirty years before launching into ministry was because He was totally satisfied just by being with His Father. When with Him, He had nowhere else to go.

Some of the Bible's greatest promises are offered to those who wait on God.

> They shall not be ashamed who wait for Me (Isaiah 49:23).
>
> For since the beginning of the world men have not heard nor perceived by the ear, nor has the eye seen any God besides You, who acts for the one who waits for Him (Isaiah 64:4).
>
> Therefore the LORD will wait, that He may be gracious to you; and therefore He will be exalted, that He may have mercy on you. For the LORD is a God of justice; blessed are all those who wait for Him (Isaiah 30:18).

I've heard it said, *You're waiting for God, but God's waiting for you*. While that may be true in some instances, that's not the point of Isaiah 30:18. Isaiah said that sometimes God will wait strategically with His answer because He wants to be even more gracious to you than if He answered right away. His delays are His kindness. He wants to give us more than a fast answer will allow. When we understand this, we're better able to wait on Him for the promised blessing.

A common idiom in American culture defines insanity as *doing the same thing but expecting a different result*. That's why, when you're waiting on God, the world calls you insane. They'll ask what has changed since you've been waiting on God. When you say, *Nothing*, they'll go, *Then do something different!* But you're not changing a thing. You understand the wisdom of waiting on God, and you refuse to be moved until God steps in with His mighty salvation.

You may wait on God for years, but in one moment of time He can change *everything*. Just ask Joseph. He waited on God for years in his prison, but when it was time for his release, God moved him from the prison to the palace in *one day*. It pays to wait on God!

Psalm 104:4 tells us the Lord *makes His ministers a flame of fire*. The word *ministers* means those who *wait on, serve, attend*. When you stand before God, wait on Him, and minister to Him, He makes *you* a flame of fire. This is what the secret place is all about. It's about waiting on the Lord, ministering to Him, and allowing Him to make us a firebrand of zeal for Jesus that burns in our generation.

A mistake King Saul made repeatedly, during his reign, was failing to wait on God. David observed and learned, and decided to do it differently. He resolved to wait on God until He spoke. As a result, David was led triumphantly from victory to victory. His story shows the wisdom of waiting on God.

That's why he left us with this advice: "Wait on the LORD; be of good courage, and He shall strengthen your heart; wait, I say, on the LORD!" (Psalm 27:14). Take it from a man who knew. When we wait on God in prayer, we give Him room to work.

CHAPTER THIRTY-THREE

The Secret of Tears

One of the most precious gifts you can bring your King is the gift of *sincerity*. Pure, wholehearted sincerity says, *Lord, I'm coming to You because You really* are *the center of my universe. You're all I live for. My heart is fully set upon You*. When you're fully given to Him, songs of abandonment flow easily from your heart, and Scriptures that help you obey are your food (Psalm 119:6).

Nothing that compromises our sincerity is worth it. Fleshly compromise—not worth it. Something that defiles our conscience—not worth it. Some worldly pleasure—not worth it.

A fully sincere heart is a precious pearl. Sell whatever you must to buy it.

Sincerity is transparent honesty, genuine purity, unsullied innocence. It has nothing to hide, and it's empowered by a clear conscience. Now, none of us are perfected yet, and all of us struggle with weakness and temptation. We're not sincere because we're without struggle; we're sincere because our reach for Jesus is wholehearted.

When your reach is passionate and blameless, I call this *sweet sincerity*. It's *sweet* because you're free from the negative traffic of a divided heart, and it's sweet because of the affections that He gives back. Here, *love is without hypocrisy* (Romans 12:9). In the sweet sincerity of true love, our awareness of His love increases. Love without hypocrisy is often accompanied by *tears*. Tears of gratefulness and longing.

Of the seven psalms that refer to tears, three are attributed to David's pen. The psalmist who had a sincere secret life with God was a man of tears. David cried, *Do not be silent at my tears* (Psalm 39:12), as though his tears commended his sincerity to God. Clearly, tears are not for women only. Yet another psalmist spoke of his tears: "My tears have been my food day and night, while they continually say to me, 'Where is your God?'" (Psalm 42:3).

Something about tears is pure and unfeigned. They're tough to fake (except by actors in movies). When someone gets teary in conversation, it stops you. Tears in the secret place are altogether honest. They get heaven's attention because they're *liquid sincerity.*

Tears make a statement to your Bridegroom. He's away, preparing for the wedding, and your tears express how much you miss Him. You long for Him and want Him to return.

Tears go where words can't.

We cry in pain, but also when overcome with delight. Tears reflect the intensity of our feelings. We long for Him to the point of pain, and delight in Him to the point of tears. Even if born in frustration and anger, tears are sweet and beautiful.

Have you known tears? You're blessed. Do you struggle to find tears? Ask for them. Ask for them *with tears.* He will answer.

One way He opens the soul's torrents is by taking us through wilderness seasons. Deprivation produces desire. He'll use famine to make us hungry, and drought to make us thirsty.

Don't despise the pain that gives you tears. Pour your heart out to Him; God is a refuge for us! Those who *love much* still wash the Lord's feet with their tears (Luke 7:36-48).

Tears get God's attention. David understood this when he wrote, *Put my tears into Your bottle* (Psalm 56:8). They're so precious to Him that He actually stores them for perpetuity.

He never forgets a single tear.

There are two kinds of God-ordained sickness in the Bible that produce tears. The first is mentioned in Proverbs 13:12, *Hope deferred makes the heart sick.* This is *heartsickness.*

When God gives you a promise of deliverance but then defers His answer, you become heartsick for His salvation. This gives you a groan in your gut and tears in your eyes. These are the tears of the brokenhearted and they're never despised by God. Heartsickness cries, *Oh God, visit me! Come to me in Your power and fulfill your word in my life!*

The other sickness that produces tears is seen in Song Of Solomon 5:8, "I charge you, O daughters of Jerusalem, if you find my beloved, that you tell him I am lovesick!" This is *lovesickness*. Lovesickness is what happens to you when your Beloved keeps His distance. You want to see Him but can't; you want to be with Him, but He still hasn't returned. *Why is this confounded veil still over my eyes? Why do I look on Him as through a dark glass? When will faith become sight?* When you've been awakened to the beauty of the King, lovesickness will express in tears. Lovesickness cries, *Show me Your glory, Lord! I want to see You and know You!*

Heartsickness is caused by unrequited power; lovesickness is caused by unrequited love.

David articulated both passions when, during his years of hiding in the wilderness, he cried, "So I have looked for You in the sanctuary, to see *Your power* and *Your glory*" (Psalm 63:2). Heartsickness weeps, *Show me Your hand!* Lovesickness weeps, *Show me Your face!*

I was once told the story of a young man in The Salvation Army who was seeking spiritual breakthrough in a certain area but had exhausted all he knew to do. He wrote General William Booth (his overseer) for advice. The General's reply was simply two words, *Try tears*.

William Booth had learned the secret. The inner chamber of prayer gains its impetus from the liquid power of tears. Never relent until you find yourself weeping in amazement as you read the Scriptures in your secret place.

Do you long for greater sincerity in your walk with God? Try tears.

CHAPTER THIRTY-FOUR

The Secret of Holiness

> Who may ascend into the hill of the LORD? Or who may stand in His holy place? He who has clean hands and a pure heart, who has not lifted up his soul to an idol, nor sworn deceitfully (Psalm 24:3-4)
>
> LORD, who may abide in Your tabernacle? Who may dwell in Your holy hill? He who walks uprightly, and works righteousness, and speaks the truth in his heart (Psalm 15:1-2).

Nothing compares to the supreme privilege of standing before the throne of God. It's the greatest of all honors and the highest of all delights. Demons envy the favor you have with Him, and angels gape in wonder at your status in His presence. And it's all because you've accepted His call to holiness. You've purified your heart, cleansed your hands, sprinkled your conscience with His blood, and clothed yourself with white robes of righteous deeds.

The Lord said, "He who walks in a perfect way, he shall serve me" (Psalm 101:6). Not that we attain sinless perfection, but we live blamelessly both before God and people. The reward of this consecration is the exhilarating privilege of standing continually in His presence.

The pursuit of holy living isn't a burden (1 John 5:3) but rather a place where we thrive and find our highest potential. Happy holiness is one of the quiet secrets of the kingdom—a purity of heart that opens to the greatest heights of communion with God.

Holiness isn't latent or inherent to us. It's derived, it's something we take on. Only God is holy in and of Himself; every other creature around His throne is holy only because they've gotten close enough that His holiness has gotten on them.

Holiness is *proximity to the throne.*

Scripture calls the creatures that surround God's throne *holy ones*. They're not holy because of *who* they are but *where* they are. They're holy by association. They minister to the Most High in the beauties of holiness, and now His holiness has made them holy.

Get in His presence, He'll make *you* holy, too. Not because of who *you* are, but because of who *He* is. Not because of *who* you are, but because of *where* you are. You minister to the Holy One and now He's making you holy.

I used to define holiness more by what we *don't* do, but now I see it derives from what we *do* do. Holiness isn't found merely by not doing the works of the world; it's found in drawing near to the holy flame on the throne. In His presence, anything unholy is burned away and all that's left is a holy, fiery love for the Son of God.

For the LORD God is a sun (Psalm 84:11). As my Sun, the Lord is my light, my warmth, and the one around whom my life revolves. His nearness brings forth fruit from the garden of my heart. His Spirit waters, His word nourishes, and His countenance warms in a way that causes the fruit of my life to grow. Like a planet around the sun, I want everything in my life to revolve around Christ. I don't want to be a comet that swings by every 300 hundred years only to return to darkness. And I don't want to be a Pluto, hanging on the furthest fringe. I want to be a Mercury—blazing with the same holy fire that radiates from His face.

Since we're on the topic of holiness, let me talk about the Holy Spirit. The *Spirit of God* was present at creation (Genesis 1:2). And in the opening books of the Bible, He's repeatedly called the *Spirit of God*. We know He's holy, but He wasn't called Holy until later. In fact, the first time He's called the *Holy Spirit* in the Bible is quite significant. It happened in the time of David.

David was a remarkable man, anointed of the Spirit, and gifted as a prophetic psalmist. He's the one who asked,

Who may dwell in Your holy hill? He devoted himself to exploring the answer. He frequently sat before the ark of the covenant, harp in hand, and Torah (his Bible) open before him. Songs would tumble and tears would flow. This is where he burned in holiness.

But David took a hard fall to sin. He committed adultery with Bathsheba and then, to hide her illegitimate pregnancy, killed her husband and married her. He seemed successful at fooling the people of his guilt, but not God. God had watched the whole thing.

David tried to pretend that he and God were still on good terms. He would grab the harp, get before the ark, and lift his voice in song. But something was terribly wrong. *The fire was gone*. Because of sin, David lost the fire of holiness. The Spirit had lifted from his life. When Nathan the prophet pointed out his sin, he repented immediately. He knew what it was to burn with a holy flame, and he longed for the flame to return. He was probably over-ready to repent.

When David repented of his sin and returned to the Lord, he wrote a song about the whole affair. Yearning to be restored to intimacy with God, David penned these words, "Do not cast me away from Your presence, and do not take Your *Holy Spirit* from me" (Psalm 51:11). When David compromised his holiness, he realized that the Spirit of God is, above all, a *Holy* Spirit. It's the first time He's called *Holy*.

The Holy Spirit dwells with those who live in holiness. Once you've experienced this fiery love in the heart, you realize that *nothing* is worth losing it!

Holiness isn't simply clean living. *Holiness is a life lived before the throne of God.*

The Scripture says of John the Baptist that, "Herod feared John, knowing that he was a just and holy man" (Mark 6:20). John was not simply a just (blameless) man; he was a holy man who lived in God's presence. Herod feared John because he was holy.

Holy people cause kings to fear. That's because they're not just pure; they're a living flame that stands at the throne of God.

If prayer is gasoline, holiness is the spark. When a holy man or woman prays, explosive things happen. Those who burn with a holy love for Jesus are influential in the courts of heaven. Like Elijah, they change things on earth by praying effective prayers that avail much (James 5:16).

God is so eager for us to find these spheres of holiness that He'll even chasten in our lives, so that *we may be partakers of His holiness* (Hebrews 12:10). At first chastening might feel damaging, but if we'll endure in love, He'll bring us through to history-changing holiness.

I want to close this chapter with this powerful truth: *Holiness produces resurrection.* As certainly as chastening produces infirmity and brokenness, holiness produces resurrection, deliverance, and healing. Our verse for this is Romans 1:4.

It says that the Lord Jesus was "declared to be the Son of God with power according to the Spirit of holiness, by the resurrection from the dead" (Romans 1:4). Paul testified that Christ's *holiness* precipitated His resurrection. This truth was prophesied in David, "For You will not leave my soul in Sheol, nor will You allow Your *Holy One* to see corruption" (Psalm 16:10). David experienced that verse in part who, being severely chastened by God, was raised up by God because of his holiness. But Jesus experienced that verse in fullness. Because of His holiness, Jesus was resurrected from Sheol. He did not see corruption—literally. He was resurrected on the third day before decay had set into His body. Jesus was the consummate fulfillment of Psalm 16:10—resurrected because He was *holy.*

It was true of David, it was true of Christ, and it's also true of you. You can't keep holiness buried forever. Even if you feel buried under the weight of God's chastening hand, devote yourself to His holy presence. Regardless of your shattered dreams and deferred hopes, live in the secret place of the Most High. It's the secret to your redemption. As you love Him from your pit, you're setting powerful spiritual forces into motion.

Joseph was buried in prison, but they couldn't keep that holy man buried forever. The longer you try to keep a holy man buried, the higher he's going to rise. Keep Joseph buried too long and he'll rise to the palace.

Death did its best to hold onto the Holy One, but by the beginning of the third day, it just couldn't hold on any longer. Death's grip gave way, and Holiness rose to the highest place:

> Therefore God also has highly exalted Him and given Him the name which is above every name, that at the name of Jesus every knee should bow, of those in heaven, and of those on earth, and of those under the earth, and that every tongue should confess that Jesus Christ is Lord, to the glory of God the Father (Philippians 2:9-11).

Regardless of the circumstances that try to bury you, live in the secret place. If you'll burn in holiness, it's inevitable—*holiness will rise again!*

CHAPTER THIRTY-FIVE

The Secret of Buying Gold

> "I counsel you to buy from Me gold refined in the fire, that you may be rich" (Revelation 3:18).

What is this gold that enriches us? It's the gold of godly character. *Christlikeness*. We all want to be conformed to the image of Christ, but there's no fast or easy way to get there. Godly character isn't *given*, it's *bought*. We buy it without money but yet at a steep price. Because gold is refined *in the fire*.

To demystify this, let me describe how we *buy gold refined in the fire*. It starts with fire. By fire, Jesus meant the heat of pressure, affliction, distress, calamity, or persecution. Peter used the term *fiery trials*. These last days will see an intense escalation of fire. You won't have to wonder whether you're in the fire. When it hits your life, you'll know it! You'll lose your sense of control, your pain levels will go through the roof, and your desperation for God will intensify.

Because your strength is limited, you'll be tempted to collapse and give up; but your spirit is alive to God, so you'll allow the fire to drive you into the face of Christ. Instead of giving up, you'll run even harder. In the fire, the secret place will be your sanity. The word will sustain your heart and the Spirit will soothe your troubled soul.

In a fiery trial, when you press into the word, it begins to read your mail. It locates you. Like a hammer, it confronts hardness in your heart (Jeremiah 23:29). It becomes a plumb line that measures your life, revealing areas of your soul that have been out of alignment with God's will. He'll show you things that need to change so you can repent (you can't repent of things you don't see).

The fire makes you zealous to repent. It makes you desperate for God and eager to do anything to increase His favor on your life. You don't just want to repent; you want to repent *deeply*. Thoughts, behaviors, motives—everything and anything is up for examination. When you're eager to change in the midst of your fiery trial, you're becoming more like Jesus. Said another way, you're buying gold in the fire.

To buy gold implies a cost. What's the cost? *Endurance*. Enduring in a trial is very costly. It means we continue to press into God—when our legs are cramping for a rest, and when our lungs are screaming at us to relax the pace. When we endure in the race, we buy gold. We'll lose things in the process, but what we gain—the knowledge of Christ—is so precious that we consider all we lost to be *rubbish* (Philippians 3:8).

The cost? Rubbish. The purchase? Gold.

When you're in the fire, it's important *how* you come to the word. You want it to confront you, challenge you, feed you, sustain you. In my case, before the fire hit my life, I would search the word for good sermon material to feed the flock I was pastoring; after the fire hit my life, I came to the word just for myself. It became personal.

God's word is a mirror (James 1:22-25). We peer into it so that, when it reflects back the things that need to change, we can repent. We don't look into the mirror to see how *others* need to change; we're only focused on the things Christ shows us about ourselves so we can embrace Spirit-empowered change. When He shows it to us, it means He's giving us grace to buy gold.

The fire will make you not just a *hearer* but a *doer* of the word (James 1:22). Let me explain. Fiery trials make you desperate for a word from God. When it comes, you cling to it like a life preserver. You know the only way that word will sustain you is if you act on it and embody it. When you're fighting to survive, you become eager to *do* the word. When you *do* it, you're buying gold.

Devotion to the word in the secret place is the only way to survive fiery trials. And when you act on His word, here's the secret: Not only will you survive, you'll overcome and buy eternal treasure. The secret place is God's ATM, the place where you access the coffers of heaven. The Lord wants you to discover this secret to true eternal treasure, and that's why He's sent this fire into your life. You're going to come through looking more like Jesus.

Nobody can steal from you gold bought in the fire. It's yours, forever.

Just your diligence to read this book is doing something within you. You're being filled with hope and energized with fresh purpose. You're receiving grace to overcome. Your weakened knees and limp hands are gaining strength, and your legs are being invigorated to chase harder after Him. You're getting it—going for the gold. You're running after Jesus in the secret place!

CHAPTER THIRTY-SIX

The Secret of Inviting His Gaze

> The LORD is in His holy temple, the LORD'S throne is in heaven; His eyes behold, His eyelids test the sons of men. The LORD tests the righteous, but the wicked and the one who loves violence His soul hates. Upon the wicked He will rain coals; fire and brimstone and a burning wind shall be the portion of their cup. For the LORD is righteous, He loves righteousness; His countenance beholds the upright (Psalm 11:4-7).

God is riveted on us. He scrutinizes and studies every move. He watches and weighs every action, attitude, and motive—because of His tender, affectionate care. He's deeply invested in us, guarding and securing our welfare. And He's ready to judge and reward every word and deed.

His eyes miss nothing.

Even if you don't want it, you have His constant gaze. You can't break free of it and you probably can't diminish it. However, you can ask for more.

Why would we want God to increase His gaze on our lives? Because His countenance represents His favor (Psalm 44:3). When Psalm 11:7 says, *His countenance beholds the upright*, you can take that to mean, *His favor is on the upright*. To put it another way, *if He likes you, He looks at you.* If you want His favor, ask Him to fasten His eyes on you.

The Lord said, "But on this one will I look: on him who is poor and of a contrite spirit, and who trembles at My word" (Isaiah 66:2). I want the Lord to look on me, so I'm fiercely committed to pursuing a poor and contrite spirit. To tremble at His word means to tremble before the authority of His word, and then tremble with eagerness to obey it. For me, this is one of the most important verses in the entire Bible.

God's eyes are on a global search. "For the eyes of the LORD run to and fro throughout the whole earth, to show

Himself strong on behalf of those whose heart is loyal to Him" (2 Chronicles 16:9). When God finds a loyal heart, it seems that His eyes cease their running and bear down with focused interest on the one who loves so devoutly. With His scrutiny comes great favor, mercy, faith, grace, compassion, and wisdom. *He shows Himself.* He shows Himself to be strong. He shows how strong He is to deliver. Yes, I want the Lord's eyes to settle on me in this way.

Wise believers—those who value kingdom treasure—will pant for this kind of attention. They'll wave and cry, *Here, Lord, I'm over here! Come and look on me!* Retreating to the secret place is like painting a bull's eye on your chest. You're doing your utmost to get heaven's attention. *Here I am, Lord. Have mercy on me and visit me. Lift up the light of Your countenance and look upon me!*

Now, here's the tricky part: His gaze is very intense. Yes, His gaze brings His favor, but He has *eyes of fire*. Fire conveys both intensity of passion and thoroughness of search. His fiery eyes can't but test you. His fire is heartwarming but also dangerously consuming. When God's fire visits your life, He's beholding you very closely. He's searching with His eyelids (Psalm 11:4). Will your heart remain loyal through the test? Persevere in love and He'll show Himself—strongly.

Saints who experience this fire can appear somewhat ambivalent. At first they cry with David, "Search me, O God, and know my heart; try me, and know my anxieties" (Psalm 139:23). But when God answers that prayer and the fire hits—whoooooooosh—they soon change their tune and sound more like Job:

> What is man, that You should exalt him, that You should set Your heart on him, that You should visit him every morning, and test him every moment? How long? Will You not look away from me, and let me alone till I swallow my saliva? Have I sinned? What have I done to You, O watcher of men? Why have You set me as Your target, so that I am a burden to myself? (Job 7:17-20).

We desire His gaze, but then when we get it, we don't want it anymore! *Will You not look away from me, and let me alone till I swallow my saliva?* The Lord is patient with us, however, and walks with us tenderly because He remembers we are dust. He's not thrown off when we're honest to His face. He's determined to finish the good work He has started in us.

Okay, so God's gaze is intense. Someone might complain, *But I don't want Him to look on me so intensely anymore.* Then consider the alternative: He can turn away from you. Now *that's* horrific!

When God said of His people, *I will hide My face from them* (Deuteronomy 32:20), it was an awful declaration of judgment. Who can imagine the dread of being separated from the light of His face? *No, Lord, do not turn away from us! Even though it means the fire of Your eyes, look on us for good. I know I asked You to look away from me, but I'm coming back to my original cry. This time I really mean it. Look on me, visit me, come to me, O consuming fire!*

I love thinking about how God concentrates His attention on us. I'm one of eight billion people on this planet, and yet He's more focused on me than I am on Him. My mind wanders away from Him all the time. For example, I get distracted by work, people, and my phone, and later realize that I haven't thought of Him for a few hours. But when my mind finally returns to Him, I realize something amazing: *He's right there!* He's been waiting for me the entire time. When my mind was disconnected, His wasn't. The Spirit is ready to renew fellowship every moment, every day. He's more intensely devoted to this relationship than I could ever be.

He *never* stops thinking about me!

His thoughts about me are more than the sand of the seashore (Psalm 139:18), and with every thought He's formulating my peaceful and hopeful future (Jeremiah 29:11). Such knowledge is too wonderful for me.

Let Him speak this word to you right now: "For I will set

My eyes on them for good, and I will bring them back to this land; I will build them and not pull them down, and I will plant them and not pluck them up" (Jeremiah 24:6).

What can I say to such kindness, Lord? Here's my simple response: "Look upon me and be merciful to me, as Your custom is toward those who love Your name" (Psalm 119:132).

When we invoke the gaze of our Beloved in this way, we step into a quiet garden of rich affection. (The secret of this chapter is tucked away right here.) We have knowledge, we understand what we're saying, but we say it anyways. *Fix Your eyes on me, altogether Lovely One!* This unyielding prayer touches Him so deeply that He responds, "You have ravished My heart, My sister, My spouse; you have ravished My heart with one look of your eyes" (Song of Solomon 4:9). Eyes locked, hearts burning…this is the secret place.

CHAPTER THIRTY-SEVEN

The Secret of The Cross

The secret place lies in the shadow of the cross. Psalm 91:1 points to this: "He who dwells in the secret place of the Most High shall abide under the shadow of the Almighty." You can't draw closer to the shadow of the Almighty than when you're clasping the cross. The cross's shadow is the saint's home.

The cross is the safest place on earth. It's where the most violent winds will lash your soul, but also where you'll enjoy the greatest immunity from Satan's devices. By taking up your cross, you're dying to every mechanism in your soul that Satan might use against you. The greatest pain produces the highest freedom. There is no strategy against crucified saints. With what can they threaten a corpse (Galatians 2:20)?

We continually return to the cross, eagerly and intentionally. We keep revisiting the crucified life because self has an uncanny way of crawling off the cross and asserting itself. The crucifixion of the self-life is not an achievement but a process: We die daily (1 Corinthians 15:31). Just as Jesus used His prayer garden (Gethsemane) to prepare for the cross, we come to the secret place to reiterate our *yes* to the Father's will, even if it involves suffering.

In our daily pilgrimage to the secret place, we wrap ourselves around His rugged tree, gaze upon His wounds, and once again die to ourselves. We accept the nails in our hands that curtail our freedoms, and we surrender to the nails in our feet that immobilize our options. We allow suffering in the flesh to cleanse us from sin (1 Peter 4:1). With dignity, we bear the honor of filling up in our flesh what is yet lacking with regard to the afflictions of Christ (Colossians 1:24).

Many see the cross as a place of pain and restriction, and

that's true. But it's so much more. It's the crux of love. The cross is the Father saying to the world, *This is how much I love you!* The cross is the Son saying to the Father, *This is how much I love You!* And the cross is the bride saying to her Bridegroom, *This is how much I love You!*

The cross is the outpouring of consummate passion. When Christ calls us to share His cross, He invites us to the highest intimacy. The wood that holds His hands now holds our hands. The nail that binds His feet to the will of God criss-crosses the nail that impales our feet to that same will. Here we hang, two lovers on opposite sides of one cross, our hearts almost touching except for the separating wood. This is our marriage bed. *Here I give Thee my troth.*

As you hang with Him here, even though your vision is clouded and you can't see His face, if you listen you'll hear His voice. With seven words He'll guide you through this dark night of your soul.

> Father, forgive them, for they do not know what they do (Luke 23:34).

Jesus begins by showing you how to forgive. This will be the first great hurdle you must cross because the wrong they committed against you was a true violation of justice. But forgiveness is the only way you'll move forward in God's purposes.

> Assuredly, I say to you, today you will be with Me in Paradise (Luke 23:43).

While your agony is fresh and raw, the Lord assures you that your name is written in heaven, and for this alone you can rejoice. The assurance of His eternal companionship carries you in this moment.

> When Jesus therefore saw His mother, and the disciple whom He loved standing by, He said to His mother, "Woman, behold your son!" Then He said to the disciple, "Behold your mother!" (John 19:26-27).

Jesus tells the church (represented by the woman) to gaze upon you in your suffering. *Behold your son!* Other believers will look on you with reproach, misunderstanding, perplexity, and inner judgments. And then He says to you, *Behold your mother, the church.* This is a time for you to look at the church and see her in a new light. As you look on her without any bitterness in your heart, you gain great wisdom in this season. What you see now will help you serve her in times to come.

> My God, My God, why have You forsaken Me? (Matthew 27:46).

You have just endured Jesus' three hours of dark silence on the cross. Now, Jesus directs you to this prayer of dereliction. You find yourself crying to God with gut-wrenching honesty. You ask all the *why* questions. Even though you know He's closer than ever, it feels like He's forsaken you. Profound intimacy and deep abandonment have kissed. You don't understand why the pain never stops.

> I thirst! (John 19:28).

Rather than cursing God in your darkness, you thirst and long for Him more than ever. Crucifixion hasn't changed anything for you because, at the end of the day, you're still saying, *I want You, Lord! You're my life. All my springs are in You.*

> It is finished! (John 19:30).

Jesus indicates that your trial is finally finished. This is the moment you've been waiting for. The work God intended in the crucible is finally complete.

Father, "into Your hands I commit My spirit" (Luke 23:46).

Jesus gently coaches you to abandon yourself to the hands of your faithful Father. As you lay your life down, He takes the profound death at work in you and transforms it into resurrection life. You're joined to Christ in His death, burial, and resurrection (Romans 6:5).

Unparalleled affection is reserved for those who share the secret place of the cross with their Beloved. Here exchanged are the fathomless passions of the Eternal God with His chosen partner. She's laying down her life for her Friend—there is no greater love (John 15:13).

Life, death, resurrection—these two do it all together. Nothing can separate them—neither death nor life nor height nor depth. Their hearts are forever entwined in the passion story of the universe. He is hers, and she is His (Song of Solomon 6:3). This is extravagant love—no length spared, no part withheld—for the cross empowers total abandonment. Every whispered *yes* stokes the flame. Anything for love!

Come aside to the desolate hill of impalement. Say *yes* yet again. Feel the cramping; sigh and groan. Join your Savior's suffering. Drink of His cup, all of it. And discover the secret of everlasting love in the shadow of the Almighty.

I take, O cross, thy shadow
For my abiding place
I ask no other sunshine than
The sunshine of His face
Content to let the world go by
To know no gain nor loss
My sinful self my only shame
My glory all the cross.
(Elizabeth C. Clephane, Public Domain)

CHAPTER THIRTY-EIGHT

The Secret of Rest

> And He said to them, "Come aside by yourselves to a deserted place and rest a while" (Mark 6:31).

The journey grew long for Jesus' disciples, and so it does for all of us. We all need, without exception, to come aside regularly for refreshment in a quiet resting place.

Rest. It's critical to long-term endurance. Jesus said He came to give us rest (Matthew 11:28), and yet Christians are some of the most overworked people on the planet. Hebrews 4 states there's a rest that remains for God's people, but it's possible to miss it. It's available but not always apprehended. To enter His rest actually requires *diligence* on our part (Hebrews 4:11). It's so valuable that we labor to find it.

Jesus designed that there be a portion of our day when we just *stop*. Refuse this role of the secret place and you're likely to struggle with the stress of life's demands. Life so easily becomes a flurry of incessant activity. Just *stop*. Get off the merry-go-round, come aside to a deserted place, and calm your heart in the love of God.

God's rest is discovered through a diligent pursuit of the secret place. We cease from our own works and learn to *be* in the presence of the Lord (Hebrews 4:10). Here is our source of rejuvenation, revitalization, invigoration, renewal.

God instituted the Sabbath (a day of rest each week) for several reasons, but one of the most compelling is found in Exodus 31:13, "Surely My Sabbaths you shall keep, for it is a sign between Me and you throughout your generations, that you may know that I am the LORD who sanctifies you." The Sabbath was *sanctifying*—making His people *different* from all other nations in the earth. Across the globe, no other nation practiced a weekly sabbath. Why not? Because they were obsessed with making money to provide their needs and get ahead in life. In contrast, Israel had one day each week in which they refused to work, but rather worshiped and rested. They were making a statement of trust in the Lord's provision. This made them different, separate, *sanctified* from others. They were a people of *faith* who were devoted to *love*. They believed God could do more to bless them in six days of labor than non-believers could obtain in seven days of unceasing toil.

Sabbath reinvigorated their physical strength, deepened their worship, and triggered greater material blessing than if they had worked seven days a week.

The people of God wore the Sabbath like a regal garment that made them stunning in the eyes of the Lord. The way they rested in His lovingkindness was simply beautiful to Him.

The Sabbath is to the week as the secret place is to the day. What I mean is, even as the Sabbath was an appointed day of rest in the course of a hardworking week, the secret place is an appointed place of rest in the course of a busy day. Our commitment to the secret place *sanctifies* us (sets us apart) to God. We're different from our unbelieving neighbors. They offer God no honor, but we take an hour every day to honor Him, commune with Him and be renewed in His rest. We believe that when we honor Him like this, He'll enable us to be more effective in 23 hours of Spirit-filled service than the 24 hours the world has without the Spirit.

What could be more therapeutic in the course of a busy day than to stop and gaze upon the glory of His majesty? If you want to see how invigorating that is, consider how John perceived the vitality of the four living creatures who serve at the throne of God. John described what he saw: "The four living creatures, each having six wings, were full of eyes around and within. And *they do not rest* day or night, saying: 'Holy, holy, holy, Lord God Almighty, who was and is and is to come!'" (Revelation 4:8). John saw them gazing on God with multitudinous eyes, and that occupation is so invigorating that they feel no need of rest, day or night, forever and ever.

Why don't the living creatures ever get tired? Because they're standing in the immediate glory of God and gazing on His beauty without veil or protective eye gear. They live in eternal rejuvenation. Instead of tiring from their service to God, they're energized and made alive by it.

The living creatures know this much better than we: Spending time in His presence doesn't diminish but enhances our productivity. It's the wellspring of Spirit empowerment. What a great secret to learn! In His presence we're at rest—we're home.

Take a few moments to talk to the Lord about your stress levels and workload. Express your resolve to come aside daily and rest in His arms. Pursue the same occupation the living creatures enjoy. Gaze upon the beauty of Jesus and be renewed in His presence. Let His glory diffuse the stress.

The Lord Jesus is giving you the secret of rest. Pursue it diligently until it's fully yours.

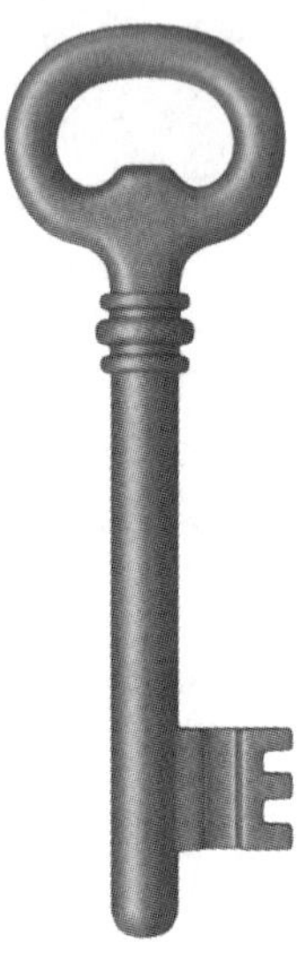

PART IV

Seeking a Deeper Relationship

Now you've come to the best part of this book. We're about to go deeper in understanding and higher in love. Let's explore high and holy truths that have the potential to carry us to new dimensions of intimacy with Christ Jesus.

CHAPTER THIRTY-NINE

The Secret of Pursuing True Riches

The Spirit of wisdom has given us the highest counsel, tucked away quietly in the book of Proverbs:

> Get wisdom! Get understanding! Wisdom is the principal thing; therefore get wisdom. And in all your getting, get understanding (Proverbs 4:5, 7).

Wisdom and understanding are pursued in the secret place by those with an eye for enduring spiritual treasure. Time spent elsewhere might enable us to earn wealth on the earthly plane, but from an eternal perspective there are things we value so much more: wisdom, understanding, and the knowledge of Christ. These are things we carry into the age to come.

When we labor for wisdom, we're pursuing Jesus Himself because *wisdom is a Person* (1 Corinthians 1:30). We're also pursuing Holy Spirit fullness, for *wisdom is a Spirit* (Isaiah 11:2). Joseph and Daniel both chased after the Spirit of wisdom and, as a result, displayed such remarkable understanding that great earthly kings brought them into their councils (Genesis 41:38; Daniel 5:11). Wisdom got them where money never could have (Proverbs 16:16).

What does it mean to be a person of understanding? The answer is in Psalm 14:2, "The LORD looks down from heaven upon the children of men, to see if there are any who understand, who seek God." The last part of the verse indicates that *to understand is to seek God.* People of understanding seek God. Anyone with half a brain will devote themselves to an abandoned pursuit of God. People who don't seek God simply don't get it. They're dull, obtuse, and playing the fool (Psalm 14:1).

People of understanding—God seekers—have come to value true spiritual treasure. They know where the *real money* is. It's found in what Jesus called *true riches*.

What did Jesus mean by that term? To answer, let's look at the verse where He coined the phrase: "Therefore if you have not been faithful in the unrighteous mammon, who will commit to your trust the true riches?" (Luke 16:11). In speaking of riches, Jesus compared the *unreliable* with the *true*, and the *temporary* with the *eternal*. In context, He was calling His followers to responsible management of financial resources. He said that if we're not faithful in our handling of unrighteous money, God won't entrust us with true riches. The unrighteous, unreliable riches were earthly money. And the true riches—what were they? Positions of honor and influence? Ministry effectiveness? Oversight of precious human souls? Those answers contain an element of truth, but they're not the highest answer.

The best answer is found later in Paul's writings: "For it is the God who commanded light to shine out of darkness, who has shone in our hearts to give the light of the knowledge of the glory of God in the face of Jesus Christ. But we have this *treasure* in earthen vessels, that the excellence of the power may be of God and not of us" (2 Corinthians 4:6-7). What is the *treasure* to which Paul refers? Answer: *the light of the knowledge of the glory of God in the face of Jesus Christ.* Summarized, true treasure is *the knowledge of Christ*.

Paul affirmed this in Colossians 2:3 when he wrote that in Christ *are hidden all the treasures of wisdom and knowledge.* In speaking of *true riches*, then, Jesus was actually speaking of Himself. True riches are *the knowledge of God.*

Jesus despised earthly riches. But He extolled the true riches of knowing God. His point in Luke 16:11 was that, when we're faithful with unrighteous money, we'll qualify for divine understanding into the beauty of the glorious Son of God, the Man Christ Jesus.

True riches are the wisdom, knowledge, and understanding of God the Father, God the Son, and God the Holy Spirit. If we have even a modicum of sense about us, we'll pursue this knowledge with abandonment. Because it's within reach. And that's where the secret place comes in. It's here—with the word open, with a heart tenderized by the Spirit, and with a panting appetite for the food of heaven—that we peer into the beauties of holiness. Our souls echo Moses' cry of long ago, "Now therefore, I pray, if I have found grace in Your sight, show me now Your way, that I may know You and that I may find grace in Your sight" (Exodus 33:13).

In kindness, the Lord has promised, "I will give you the treasures of darkness and hidden riches of secret places, that you may know that I, the LORD, who call you by your name, am the God of Israel" (Isaiah 45:3). Originally, this was a promise to Cyrus that he would uncover the hidden treasures buried in Egypt's pyramids. Applied to us today, we're assured there are great riches to be mined in the secret place of the Most High. *Go to work and ferret out the nuggets hidden in the recesses of God's richly-laden word.*

May God give you an eye for the true riches hidden in Christ, and a hunger to seek them out. When you're in your secret place, may He grant you the Spirit of wisdom and revelation to know Christ more. Paul's prayer about this is worth reviewing one more time:

> Therefore I also…do not cease to give thanks for you, making mention of you in my prayers: that the God of our Lord Jesus Christ, the Father of glory, may give to you the spirit of wisdom and revelation in the knowledge of Him, the eyes of your understanding being enlightened; that you may know what is the hope of His calling, what are the riches of the glory of His inheritance in the saints, and what is the exceeding greatness of His power toward us who believe (Ephesians 1:15-19).

CHAPTER FORTY

The Secret of Beholding Jesus

Some folks read the Bible to learn truths, insights, or principles. However, coming to the Bible with your head can leave your heart untouched. Scripture gives us so much more than just truth about God—it shows the way to know Him personally. As we behold Him in the word, we come to know Him in a way that sets our hearts on fire.

If you're not distracted by Him you're not seeing Him.

The Pharisees made a disastrous error in their approach to Scripture. They dissected it analytically but didn't pursue the heart and intentions undergirding the truth. Thus, they came to know the Book but not the Author. Jesus pointed to this when He said, "You search the Scriptures, for in them you think you have eternal life; and these are they which testify of Me. But you are not willing to come to Me that you may have life" (John 5:39-40). Everything they read in the Scriptures was shouting, *See your Messiah as you read, see Jesus!* But they missed it.

Scripture has always sought to direct our attention to a *Person*. Paul said *the purpose of the commandment is love* (1 Timothy 1:5); that is, the principal purpose of the Old Testament was to enflame hearts with love for God. They got stuck on dogma and creed, however, and missed the living relationship that He longed to have with them.

Jesus' words to the Pharisees raise a frightening possibility: We can study the Bible and never get to know the Lord. Even though Jesus is revealed on almost every single page, it's possible to read the words and never develop a burning-heart relationship with Him. He was saying we ought not come to the Scriptures to gain knowledge about spiritual truths; rather, we should come to the Scriptures to gain knowledge about He who is Truth. The Living Word wants to meet us in the

Written Word, if we'll only look for Him.

Here's the secret: Your reading in the word is meant to be a dynamic encounter with the person of the Lord Jesus Christ. Don't do Bible reading as a rote way to knock off your daily quota of chapters, or merely a way to glean spiritual principles and read interesting stories. Rather; come to gaze upon the majesty and mystery of the One who has captured your heart—the altogether Lovely One. He waits for you behind the veil, watching to reward those who pant for Him as for springs of living water. Come with a cry in your heart to see Him and know Him. All the Holy Spirit has to do is breathe on one tiny word of Scripture and your heart will race with fresh revelation, faith, and affection.

When Jesus joined the two disciples walking to Emmaus after His resurrection, He explained to them how He was the central theme of the Scriptures. Imagine the glory of this encounter—Jesus revealing Jesus to the heart from the written word! When they debriefed about it later, they said, "Did not our heart burn within us while He talked with us on the road, and while He opened the Scriptures to us?" (Luke 24:32). What caused their hearts to burn? Fresh revelation into who Jesus is, as seen in the Scriptures through the power of the Holy Spirit. Our hearts are set on fire the same way. Our hope for *opened Scriptures* keeps us returning to the secret place.

Jesus is seen even in the Bible's miracles, signs, wonders, and stories. Whenever you see Him exercising His power, something is revealed about who He is. This is the testimony of Psalm 9:16, *The LORD is known by the judgment He executes*. A judgment is a decision to act in a certain way. Whenever God decides to exercise action in a situation, He's revealing something about Himself. The wise study His works because, in doing so, they come to know Him more. The miracle stories of the Bible reveal *so* much about your Beloved!

My heart cries, *I want to know You, Lord! I want to behold You in Your word. I want to know Your power until faith fills every atom of my being; and I want to know Your glory until love flows through my heart like a torrential river. Manifest Yourself to me in Your word, O Lord!* This is my foremost secret place cry. With David I ache, *Oh, when will You come to me?* (Psalm 101:2).

In my personal experience, I haven't come to know Jesus better just in prayer. Let me explain. For me, prayer is a time for me to express my love and receive His. It's where love is expressed and exchanged. But *to get to know Him better*, I go to the word. To know more of Christ requires revelation, and revelation requires meditation in the word. For me, beholding Jesus happens when I'm *praying in the word*. That's where I experience 2 Corinthians 3:18, "But we all, with unveiled face, beholding as in a mirror the glory of the Lord, are being transformed into the same image from glory to glory, just as by the Spirit of the Lord."

I'm so eager to behold Him that I must confess to a little bit of holy jealousy when I think about how the living creatures behold Him 24/7. They never turn to the side, no matter where they go, but always face straight ahead—never taking their eyes off the throne (Ezekiel 1:12-17). They have the glorious privilege of gazing eternally upon the beauty of the King. Lord, this is how I want to live my eternity, too. No matter where I go or what I do, may my eyes always be fastened upon You and Your radiant majesty.

The more I see of Jesus in His word, the more I realize how different He is from me. And His uniqueness is the very thing that pulls me in. I've discovered that I'm naturally attracted to that which is different from me (as the saying goes, opposites attract). *Ain't nobody like Jesus!* He sets my heart to pounding. I'm going to take advantage of the privilege the secret place provides me—the privilege of gazing on Jesus in the Scriptures. I'm on an everlasting adventure of growing in the knowledge of Him who died for me.

Jesus, we're back in the secret place—again—because we have eyes only for *You*.

CHAPTER FORTY-ONE

The Secret of Standing

When you're in the secret place, you're in the company of saints and angels who stand on the sea of glass and gaze upon the throne (Revelation 15:2). Your eyes are veiled and you can't actually see Him. But you know, by faith, that you're with them before the throne. Standing here and burning with holy affections before your burning God is your eternal destiny. Every time you shut your door and stand before God, you taste a little of heaven on earth.

You stand here in the face of much opposition. Your schedule doesn't want to give you room for this; your body clock complains; work and family demands tell you that you don't have time for this; and, of course, all of hell wars against your stand. But you've awakened to the beauties of holiness and won't allow anything to rob you of this privilege. Just to stand before God; and having done all, to stand!

To stand, despite the warfare; to stand, despite the resistance; to stand, despite the hassles; to stand, despite the weariness; to stand, despite the distresses; to stand, despite the temptations; to stand, despite personal failure and collapse; to stand, despite the grief; to stand, despite the loneliness; to stand, even when chained; just to stand!

To stand, because of the cross; to stand, because of the Lamb; to stand, because of His affections; to stand, because of His acceptance; to stand, because of His mighty power within; to stand, because of fountains of living water flowing up from within; to stand, because of His surpassing beauty and greatness; to stand, because of His eternal purpose; to stand, because of His everlasting mercies; to stand, because of love; just to stand!

The Levites' job description is still applicable to us today: "At that time the LORD separated the tribe of Levi to bear the ark of the covenant of the LORD, to stand before the LORD to minister to Him and to bless in His name, to this day" (Deuteronomy 10:8). Our greatest responsibility and privilege is to stand before the Lord and minister to Him. In the secret place we simply stand. No great agenda, no mighty ambitions, no rush to move on to the next thing. We just stand before Him, love Him, and enjoy Him.

There are seasons when God calls us to simply stand. We might prefer the adrenalin of chasing down a great cause, but sometimes God calls us to stop the activity and just stand. Sometimes, we have no choice. Occasionally, circumstances will restrict our options and chain us to God's will. Incapable of extricating ourselves from our place of confinement, all we can do is stand and burn in holy love for the King.

A common American dictum goes, *Don't just stand there, do something!* The idea is, when you don't know what to do, don't just stand around doing nothing; find *something* to do. This idea sometimes leaks over into our walk with Christ. When facing circumstances we can't control, we're often tempted to come up with *something* to do. We've been told, *God can't steer a stationary vehicle*, so we'll step out and start to do *something*, hoping God will step in and direct our course.

That may be a good approach in some situations, but the Lord has been leading in my life in a different way. He inverted that common saying and gave it to me this way: *Don't just do something, stand there!* It came like this: *When you don't know what to do, don't just do something. Wait on Me, stand before Me, minister to Me, until. Until I speak. When I show the way forward, then you can move in response. But until I speak, stand there.*

I stand before the Lord like David, who said, *I have set the LORD always before me* (Psalm 16:8). Like the Levites, I bear His presence on my shoulders, I stand before Him to minister to Him, and I bless others in His name (Deuteronomy 10:8). This is my glorious occupation, to stand before Him, gaze upon His beauty, and bless Him while I have breath.

To stand before God in this way, we can learn something from the angels. For example, consider the angel Gabriel. Gabriel made three appearances in Scripture. The first was when he appeared to Daniel. The second was almost 600 years later when he came to tell Zacharias that he would beget John the Baptist. His third visit was six months later, when he announced to Mary her impregnation by the Holy Spirit.

Let's talk about Gabriel's visit to Zacharias. When he delivered God's message, Zacharias couldn't believe his words. In the context of the conversation, the angel reinforced the authority of his words by declaring, "I am Gabriel, who stands in the presence of God" (Luke 1:19).

Someone might wonder, *So what do you do, Gabriel?*

I stand in the presence of God.

Yes, we understand that, but what do you do?

Actually, I stand in the presence of God.

Yes, yes, Gabriel, we understand that. But you're such a powerful angel. I mean, what does a mighty angel like you DO??

Gabriel would say, *This is what I do. I stand in the presence of God. I stand there, beholding His majesty and splendor, exhilarated by the wonder of who He is, and wait upon Him until He speaks. If He says nothing, I just stand there. When He gives a word, then I move to fulfill it. But mostly I just stand before Him and minister to Him.*

Between Daniel and Zacharias is a 600-year period during which we hear nothing from Gabriel; then between Zacharias and Mary was a 6-month period. That was the busy season. What did Gabriel do between assignments? He just stood.

Sometimes God is wasteful. He'll have a mighty angel like Gabriel just standing for centuries at a time. God has legions of powerful angels at His disposal, and with a small signal He could send any of them to change human history in the flash of a moment. But instead of sending them on a mission to earth, what does He have them doing? Just standing at the throne. Seems such a waste of power.

Sometimes God also seems to be wasteful with us. For example, imagine a believer who is faithful to cultivate their gifts, talents, and strengths, until they become a finely tuned instrument of ministry potential. Once they're ready to be deployed to do great exploits for the kingdom, what does He do next? He takes that well-oiled ministry machine, places it on a shelf, and says, *Stand there.*

This is what God did with Elijah. Elijah did so much standing that he developed an expression for it: "As the LORD God of Israel lives, before whom I stand" (1 Kings 17:1). Elijah claimed, *I stand before God. That's what I do.* And that claim certainly got tested along the way.

For example, it got tested when he was holed up for three years in a widow's house. The nation was under a famine at Elijah's command, and King Ahab was searching everywhere for him. Elijah couldn't even stick his head out the door—for three years. He was literally under house arrest in a hot, stuffy, bleak little hut. No friends, no visiting prophets, no other voices to comfort or give him perspective. And the food? Fry cakes for breakfast, fry cakes for lunch, and more of the same for supper. I can suppose Elijah thinking, *Lord, why do You have me holed up in this widow's house? This is such a waste! Look at all the ministry potential you're squandering here. I mean, I'm Elijah! In the last three years, I could have graduated an entire class in the School Of The Prophets. We could be taking the nations by storm. But no, here I stand and rot.*

Actually, I don't think Elijah felt that way. He had been trained in the Spirit to stand before God. When stuck in a house for three years, he just continued to do what he always did anyways. He stood before God and ministered to Him. *This is who I am and this is what I do.*

If God ever needs someone strong to do something, He's

got all the strength He needs immediately available to Him—mighty angels just standing around His throne and waiting for a word. As I pondered that reality, the Holy Spirit whispered to me, *I don't need your strength.* He's not needing our strength, He's looking for our availability. In the secret place, we simply make ourselves available. We stand before Him, love Him, and fulfill His word when He speaks.

Are you between assignments? Then stand. Enjoy Him and let Him enjoy you.

CHAPTER FORTY-TWO

The Secret of Bodily Light

We know that Jesus came to give us light in our spirit, soul, and mind. But it's interesting to notice that He also came to give us light in our *body*:

> No one, when he has lit a lamp, puts it in a secret place or under a basket, but on a lampstand, that those who come in may see the light. The lamp of the body is the eye. Therefore, when your eye is good, your whole body also is full of light. But when your eye is bad, your body also is full of darkness. Therefore take heed that the light which is in you is not darkness. If then your whole body is full of light, having no part dark, the whole body will be full of light, as when the bright shining of a lamp gives you light (Luke 11:33-36).

Jesus framed this fascinating idea that our bodies can be filled with either light or darkness. The secret place seems to play a critical role, and the implications affect our joy, confidence, authenticity, and impact on others. I have only a tiny bit of insight into this truth, so I hope this chapter whets your appetite to search it out further.

There's a place to attain in God in which His light so fills us that it shines throughout our entire bodies. It's a place of increased freedom from the power of sin and temptation. Temptation sometimes finds its power by appealing to dark areas within our body. When the body is full of light, bodily sins lose their power over us and we walk in greater levels of victory.

Not *all* sins are *bodily sins*. For example, hatred or rage are not sins of the body but of the soul. *Bodily sins* are committed with our bodies, such as drunkenness, gluttony, fornication, masturbation, viewing pornography, illegal drug usage, murder, stealing, lying, slander, coarse language. When God's light increases in our bodies, we're strengthened to overcome bodily sins.

How do we get greater light into our body? Through the eye. Jesus said a good eye will bring light into the body and a bad eye will keep it out. The whole thing has to do with the *eyes*.

We come to the secret place to see the light of God's word (Psalm 119:105). If our eye is clear and healthy, God's word will illumine every corner of our hearts, minds, and bodies and we'll be filled with light and truth throughout our entire being. It seems that the health of our eyes is determined by the things we look at. If we'll use our eyes to peer into the law of liberty (God's word), we'll be filled with understanding and our eyes will be bright; if we allow our eyes to look at things that defile, our minds will be contaminated, our bodies will be havens for darkness, and our eyes will become clouded.

Guard your eyes, dearly beloved! Reserve them for His word and face. Then, when temptation comes, your body won't fight against your spirit. Your body will be aligned with light, and your hands, stomach, and tongue will be devoted to righteousness instead of sins that enslave.

A reader once wrote to a certain Christian magazine editor, confessing his struggles with his thought life. He was asking for help in his battle against lust. The editor's glib response was basically, *Lighten up, you're too hard on yourself. There are healthy ways to enjoy beautiful women without wanting them.* I was dumbfounded. The editor's offhand response did nothing to equip the brother for warfare against bodily sins. How I wished for him to hear, *Check your eyes! What are you looking at? Consecrate your eyes to gaze only on the word of God and your body will fill with light.*

When our eye is bad, we can come to God's word and still not see much. We must do more than stop looking at wrong things—we must put salve on our eyes so we might see right things. As Jesus said, "Anoint your eyes with eye salve, that you may see" (Revelation 3:18). What is this eye salve? I believe we apply salve to our eyes through the spiritual disciplines of fasting, prayer, study of Scripture, almsgiving, forgiveness, etc. *The commandment of the Lord enlightens the eyes* (Psalm 19:8). As we devote ourselves to God's word in a disciplined, devout way, our eye will slowly begin to clear and allow the light of Christ into our bodies. *Pursue clear eyes.*

Victory over sin is not the only reward of a body filled with light. Of even greater significance is the intimacy we find with Christ. When our body is full of light, it aligns with His will and makes us clear channels of grace. This strengthens our sense of *sweet sincerity*—which is the boldness we gain in His embrace because of a confident conscience.

When you approach the Lord with a body full of light, you don't need a "warm up period" before you feel free to worship. No, you're *continually fervent in spirit* (Romans 12:11). You're ready at any moment to soar in worship with Jesus.

Look again at how the Lord began His teaching on bodily light. He said, "No one, when he has lit a lamp, puts it in a secret place or under a basket, but on a lampstand, that those who come in may see the light" (Luke 11:33). When our eye is good and our whole body is full of light, we shine with a radiance we ourselves may not even realize. Truth and righteousness have us lit up like a shining lamp! When He has brightened you with this kind of light, He won't bury your witness in a place of obscurity. Rather, He said He'll place that kind of light on a lampstand so that *everyone coming into the house may see the light*.

In summary, therefore, when your body is full of light, you'll know greater victory over bodily sins, you'll touch deeper dimensions of intimacy with Jesus, and you'll be granted a place of greater influence in the body of Christ. What a powerful thing to pursue in the secret place: good, clear eyes that fill your body with light.

Our generation needs you to *shine*!

CHAPTER FORTY-THREE

The Secret of Just Loving Him

God gave His only begotten Son, and Jesus died an excruciating death, all for love. The central reason for this whole thing between God and man is love. He's looking for love. He didn't die to enlist your strength in His army—He already has more than enough power to vanquish every foe. He didn't die for you because He was lonely and looking for companionship—He's surrounded in glory by multiplied millions of creatures. Rather, He died for one all-encompassing reason—to express the lengths of His love for us, and in turn awaken in us extravagant affections for Him. *He did it all for love.*

Love is the primary staple of the secret place. Much of your quiet time will likely be given simply to the exchange of affection. You'll find thousands of ways to say *I love You*, and He'll stun and satisfy you with the many ways He reciprocates His passions for you.

Start your day with just loving Him. Your requests can wait; Bible study can wait; intercession can wait. Before anything else, tell Him over and over, *I love You*. Remind Him that you, also, are in it only for love. *I'm here with my door shut, Father, because I love You. You're the center of my universe. I admire and reverence Your name. I just like being with You.*

The Lord has put His requirements within easy reach of every one of us, regardless of social class, age, personality, or ethnicity. All He wants is love. Even the mentally disabled are often capable of this. Love is the great equalizer, putting us all on the same level. No one has an advantage over another in giving and receiving love.

Don't try to be intellectually stimulating to Jesus. There's nothing you could say that would cause Him to go, *Wow, I've never seen it like that before!* Your mental prowess doesn't add any value to His life. He enjoys you, not because you're quick and witty, but because you're heartfelt, sincere, visceral, authentic, and relational. Just come and love Him.

On the other hand, don't be discouraged if you feel like an intellectual dullard. Even if your mental processor runs at a slow speed, He loves your love. He's not bored with you because you're an uneducated, simple pilgrim. In fact, He prefers childlikeness. He's not looking for elegant words but a simple and heartfelt *I love You*. Your love is as endearing to Him as that of a genius.

In the secret place, we exercise ourselves to become better lovers of God. We practice the language of love; we surrender to the Spirit of love; we search for ways to give even more of our hearts to Him in love. This is true regardless of our personality. Whether we're more emotional by temperament or analytical by nature, we can love. And we can grow in expressing it better.

Let me speak as a father for a moment. The times I enjoy my kids most are when they're enjoying my company or expressing their affection to me. They don't try to express their love with fancy words. They might even feel clumsy or unsure of how to express themselves. Maybe all they know to do in the moment is show love with a kiss or a touch or a gesture. However they show it, their simplest expressions satisfy my heart.

I think our heavenly Father feels the same toward us. He loves it when we're free to be ourselves in His presence and childlike in our affections.

As you express your love to the Lord, you may find yourself wanting to sing. The secret place is perfect for love songs because He's the only one listening. Here you can express yourself freely to your Friend, knowing that He's not distracted with your pitch or vibrato or rhythmic meter. All He hears is your heart. He receives your song as the finest solo. In fact, I hear Him saying to you right now, *I wish you'd sing to Me more often.*

There's something symbiotic about music and love. Listen to the music on a radio station and chances are that 95% of the songs have to do with love. Music and love, they go together. That's why music and singing are often a natural part of our secret life with God. Let your songs be for His ears only. Explore the holy delights of singing psalms, hymns, and spiritual songs to your Beloved (Ephesians 5:19). The Spirit will help you use song to soar in love.

Paul wrote about being *rooted* in love (Ephesians 3:17). When you give Him your love, you're putting down roots into His love. A strong root system in love will make you so confident in love that no storm will be able to uproot you. Satan will try to blow you over with winds of adversity, but you're rooted and grounded in love. Through your secret life with God, you've become established in love. Even though the love of many will grow cold (Matthew 24:12), it will not come near you because you're rooted in a love that will never let you go.

Oh, dear friend, are you established in the Father's love? As His word is open before you, does your heart move in affection for the Lamb of God? Has love settled your heart? He loves you with an everlasting love (Jeremiah 31:3). He has literally killed Himself to be joined to you. His love is so breathtaking, so vast, so intoxicating that, when you're filled with it, you're being *filled with all the fullness of God* (Ephesians 3:16-19). What a glorious adventure, to explore the magnificent magnitude of Christ's boundless love!

I cherish the powerful assurance of Psalm 91:14, "Because he has set his love upon Me, therefore I will deliver him." As someone who needs His deliverance, I've decided to set my love upon Him every day, regardless of circumstances or emotions. As I love Him in the secret place, I know He's working even the difficult circumstances together for good

(Romans 8:28). He's my Deliverer, and He's going to deliver me. O how I love Him!

I remember a five-year period of struggle during which all I could do was fall on my face and say, *I love You*. I couldn't do any spiritual warfare; I couldn't do any intercession; I couldn't fight any battles. All I could do was love. In retrospect, I now realize I actually *was* doing spiritual warfare because, when you love Him in your darkness, you're exercising the most violent kind of warfare possible. Love is the most powerful force in the universe. When you simply love Him, you're stepping into a dimension where He fights for those He loves.

I hope you're latching onto this awesome secret. *Just love Him!* Open the alabaster jar of your heart and pour yourself at His feet in loving adoration. After all, it was love that brought you to this moment in the first place. It *was* about love, it *is* about love, and it *will be* about love. Sing it, say it, pray it, *I love You*.

And then receive His love—until you're filled with all the fullness of God.

CHAPTER FORTY-FOUR

The Secret of Being Known

Some people may ask, *Do you know God?* But a far more important question is: *Does God know you?* The issue on the day of judgment will not be whether you know Him but whether He knows you.

Many will claim to know God on that day. They'll say, "Lord, Lord, I know You! I have prophesied in Your name, baptized people in Your name, cast out demons and healed many people in Your name. I swear I *do* know You!"

But to some He will reply, "I don't know you, and I don't know where you're from. In fact, I *never* knew you. Depart from Me, you who practice lawlessness!" (See Matthew 7:21-23 and Luke 13:25-27.)

No words could possibly be more terrifying to hear! How horrifying to *think* you know God, only to discover that He doesn't know you. How dreadful to be told your connection to Him was only a pretentious, public thing with no private friendship behind it. The implications here are eternal, so there can be no more fundamentally important question than this: What must I do to be known by God?

The answer has everything to do with our secret life in God. He wants us to unveil ourselves in the secret place (2 Corinthians 3:18), remove every façade, and lay bare the innermost secrets of our heart. The good, the bad, the ugly—all of it.

He wants love that withholds nothing—a relationship of total transparency and honesty. When I allow Him to see the naked truth about my brokenness, carnality, and deep inner longings, He responds by changing me—more and more each day—into the image of Christ.

"But," someone might counter, "Do we really have to talk

about the dark stuff? I thought God already knows everything about us anyways."

Yes, He does. He knows the darkness of our hearts better than we. But just because He sees the dark rooms of our hearts doesn't mean His light has been invited into those places.

Ever since Adam and Eve, we've been hiding and covering up. When we try to conceal our condition from Him, we not only deceive ourselves but draw back from letting Him know us. For Him to know us, we must expose to Him all our thoughts, motives, desires, and actions. When we come to Him like an open book, His grace empowers us to overcome sins that had previously seemed unconquerable.

Prayer is a relationship in which we allow Him to see what we'd rather cover up, and touch what we'd rather hide.

Judas Iscariot is a sobering example of a man who was in Jesus' inner circle but didn't allow Jesus into the secrets of his heart. In the light of day, he multiplied bread, healed the sick, and cast out demons. But in the darkness of his heart, he was filled with covetousness that had turned him into a compulsive thief. He could have brought it into the light and confessed it to Jesus at any time. In fact, over the course of three years, Jesus gave him many opportunities to do so. Instead, he stuffed it down and chose repeatedly to hide, hide, hide. Eventually, Satan was able to take hold of that stronghold in Judas's life and pull him to his destruction. His story illustrates the terrifying possibility that we can spend lots of time in the group with Jesus and still not be known by Him.

Jesus can handle knowing our struggles; what He won't tolerate is when we pretend they don't exist. *The secret place is no place for secrets.* It's where we reach for Him with complete honesty and full disclosure.

And here's the awesome part: When we confess our struggles and step into the light, He lavishes us with acceptance, forgiveness, dignity, and power to overcome. He's like, *You're willing to confess everything? Then I'm willing to confess you before My Father and all the holy angels, and claim you as My own.* Wow! I was afraid that if He knew *the real me*, He'd reject me; turns out, He does the exact opposite. When I let Him see all of me, He immerses me in love, grace, identity, and confidence.

When you see how completely Jesus accepts you, it inspires you to open every crevice of your heart to His gaze.

And *that's* where the intimacy is! Where nothing is withheld. Where He knows us, and we know Him. At the cross, He abandons Himself to us and gives us the grace to abandon ourselves to Him. We give everything—and then we keep searching for ways to give even *more.* We want to know and be known.

It's a wonderful thing to be known—to feel like, *He gets me.* He knows me, understands me, and enjoys me. Bill Gaither put this line into one of his songs, *The one who knows me best loves me most.*

One reason we delight in Christ's leadership is because He never misunderstands us. It's frustrating to be misunderstood—to think a certain way about a situation, but have others misinterpret your intentions and draw a wrong conclusion about you. We feel misunderstood and maybe even violated when others wrongly judge our motives. That never happens with Jesus, however. He knows what's motivating us because He knows our hearts.

The twelve disciples felt safe under Jesus' leadership because, even when He corrected them, He addressed their issues in a way they felt understood. They didn't need to pretend or perform to be loved. Their motives were completely understood but yet they felt unconditionally loved. They experienced *being known by God.*

David wrote, *You have known my soul in adversities* (Psalm 31:7). God uses adversity to find out who we really are. Pain peels away the pretenses. We don't enjoy trials, but they are often catalysts to being known more fully by God.

Paul wrote, *But if anyone loves God, this one is known by Him* (1 Corinthians 8:3). When we love Him in every season of life—even in tough times—He embraces us and knows us. Nothing is more dignifying than having a knowing relationship with God Almighty.

Jesus, know me. I'm going to keep loving You in the secret place because I want to know You and be known by You.

CHAPTER FORTY-FIVE

The Secret of Intimacy First

The first thing is the great thing—to love God with all our heart. It's our greatest commandment (Matthew 22:37-38), and it's our first priority (Revelation 2:4). Loving God comes first, even before serving others.

Serving others is the second commandment. Jesus said it's *like* the first commandment in that it's dear to God's heart, and yet He clearly placed it second (Matthew 22:39). It's a real *close* second and almost inseparable from the first, but it's still second.

We must keep *first things first*. When loving God gets our first strength, we'll live in spiritual health and have the inner reserve to execute the second commandment well. But when our priorities get backwards and we give our first strength to serving people, we're likely to over-extend, burn out, or malfunction. We're designed by our Maker to work right only as we to keep returning to our first love.

The Holy Spirit is in the business of restoring the first commandment to first place in our lives. When Jesus is our first love, we find security and identity in Him. As we stand before Him in love, we find out who we really are. He wants us to find our identity, not primarily in what we do for Him (the second commandment), but in who we are in His presence (the first commandment).

I'm not primarily a worker for God; first and foremost, I'm a child of God. I'm a son first and a soldier second. Love comes before labor. That order is vitally important. If necessary, the Holy Spirit is willing to turn our lives right-side-up so we get first things first again. By the time He's finished correcting us, *we'll be lovers who work rather than workers who love.*

In the secret place, we find our identity before the throne of God. Here, being close to Jesus becomes our primary occupation. This is where love is incubated and grown. We can't develop intimacy on the run. We have to stop, pull up to the table, lay out the bread and cup, and dine together.

It's great to enjoy His presence while driving to work, but if your commute to and from work is your only secret place opportunity, you'll miss the deeper pleasures of undistracted intimacy. You can't go deep on the fly.

Speaking from personal experience, I know what it's like to get the two great commandments inverted without even realizing it. There came a time when the Lord pulled me up short and kindly showed me how my life priorities were imbalanced. He said, *Bob, you come to Me like to a gas station.* Now, I view a gas station as a necessary evil. I don't like to fill up with gas, I like to drive. But I know that if I'm going to do what I *really* want to do (drive), I've got to gas up. The Holy Spirit was showing me that I came to the secret place in the same way. I came aside to pray in order to get filled up. Once filled, I was relieved when my prayer time was over because now I could do what I *really* wanted to do—drive my ministry machine.

The Lord seemed to be saying, *You don't come to Me because I'm your first love; you come to Me to get recharged so you can pursue the first love of your life.* Suddenly, I saw that my first love was serving people. I loved to drive! I wanted to see souls saved; I wanted to win my city for Christ; I wanted to change the world. I was motivated more by doing stuff for Him than by being with Him. I claimed, *All my springs are in You* (Psalm 87:7), but in fact I found my greatest sustenance in accomplishing kingdom exploits. And I didn't even realize it until He showed it to me.

When I saw this, my soul was deeply injured. I collapsed in pain and cried, *Lord, I'm sorry, this isn't how I want it to be. I don't want a filling station relationship with You. I want it to be about love! I want our romance to be so real that being with You in the secret place is what I live for. I want to enjoy being with You so much that they have to drag me out of the secret place!*

I sensed the Lord responding, *Yes, son, I know that's what you want. And that's why I've revealed your heart. That's why I've allured you into this wilderness (Hosea 2:14). I'm awaking you to a love deeper than what you knew in your younger, busier years.*

The Lord has many ways to correct our priorities. In my case, He simply removed my ministry. O how it hurt! I wondered, *Lord, why does this hurt so much? You haven't removed Your presence from my life; all You've done is remove my ministry. And I'm a ball of pain. Why does it hurt so much?* He was gentle in answering, but showed me the second commandment had become my first fountain. In showing this to me, He was inviting me to get it right—to place the first commandment back in first place. I learned, all over again, the joy of coming to the secret place simply to be with Him.

He wants us addicted, not to the wine of ministry but to the wine of His love (Song of Solomon 1:2). Ministry can be intoxicating. There's a certain *buzz* you feel when the grace of God flows through you and helps people. It's satisfying to watch their faces light up with the glory of God because of the way you're serving them. It feels significant because the fruit is eternal. You sense that God has honored your obedience. And all the talents you've cultivated and developed are impacting lives. Something inside you goes, *This is it! This is what I was created for. I've found my niche. This is my calling and ministry. Now I know my place in the body. I don't think I'll ever weary of serving the body of Christ in this way.*

Now, there's nothing wrong with enjoying ministry. In fact, God wants you to—as long as the second commandment stays in second place. But we're easily inebriated with the wine of *doing*, when He wants us satisfied with the wine of His love—the wine of *being*. Being with Him.

So He comes to us, like He did to the Ephesians who were so successful in ministry, and says, *I'm calling you back to your first love* (Revelation 2:4). He wants people of *one thing*: the passionate pursuit of His face. That's what David was after, for he wrote, "*One thing* I have desired of the LORD, that will I seek: that I may dwell in the house of the LORD all the days of my life, to behold the beauty of the LORD, and to inquire in His temple" (Psalm 27:4). In the same spirit, Paul said, "But *one thing* I do," which was pursuing "the upward call of God in Christ Jesus" (Philippians 3:13-14). Likewise, Mary of Bethany discovered that, "*One thing* is needed" (Luke 10:42)—to sit at Jesus' feet and hear His word. David's one thing was Paul's one thing was Mary's one thing. It's the first commandment in first place, the pursuit of a loving relationship with our beautiful Bridegroom.

All hell will militate against your becoming a man or woman of one thing. Circumstances will go haywire; your to-do list will mushroom; the demands on your life will escalate. Satan will employ any device—anything to keep you from becoming a person of one thing. Because if you find this, you'll become a blazing torch for God. Love for Jesus will empower and energize everything you do.

When we get the first commandment in first place, we become dangerous weapons in His hand for end-time exploits.

When we find our sense of fulfillment and success from the affections He gives in the secret place, we're freed from the tyranny of the ups and downs of serving. Whether our service is well received or not, we're successful on the inside because of love. We're stabilized and anchored by the power of an inner life with God. This liberates us to obey the second command more lavishly than ever by laying our lives down for others. When intimacy is first, we're empowered to serve more extravagantly than ever.

In closing, look at Matthew 5:15, "Nor do they light a lamp

and put it under a basket, but on a lampstand, and it gives light to all who are in the house." God wants to light your lamp with a blazing zeal for the face of Christ. He wants the reality of your relationship to be a light that shines to everyone around you. When your love is white-hot, pure, bright, and clean, He won't hide that kind of a lamp under a basket. Instead, He'll set you on a lampstand to give light to the entire household of faith.

Some of the most gifted ministries have been placed under a basket and limited to a localized orb of influence because the Lord wasn't willing to export the mixture in their love to the wider body of Christ.

May you learn the secret of loving Jesus first and foremost, and may He see fit to place your lamp on a lampstand. May the simplicity and purity of your devotion be an inspiration to your generation. Amen.

CHAPTER FORTY-SIX

The Secret of Bridal Identity

I think turtledoves are beautiful birds with their glossy gray feathers, dark eyes, and noble poise. They're not a nervous bird, but have a calm disposition. You'll usually find them in pairs because they mate for life.

While driving down the highway one day, I noticed two turtledoves waddling onto the road ahead of me. I don't swerve for birds or animals and, since I was doing 50 MPH, I thought to myself, *Those birds better get off the road or I'll hit them.* Sure enough, by the time they saw me and started to move it was too late. THWAP! There were feathers everywhere. I hit them both. I thought to myself, *Stupid birds. They should have moved sooner.* It was later I learned something about doves: they tend to have tunnel vision on what's before them. They were too distracted with each other to notice the oncoming vehicle. The lovebirds didn't even see me coming!

Jesus is our Bridegroom, and in the Song of Solomon He says to His bride, *You have dove's eyes* (Song of Solomon 1:15). Jesus and His bride are like a pair of turtledoves. We're always together, in covenant for life, and can't peel our eyes off each other. He whispers to us, *You have dove's eyes. You have tunnel vision for Me only. You're not distracted with other affections. Your gaze is on Me only, and I love that!*

I'm His bride. You're His bride. Together, we're His bride. As such, our love for Jesus involves *romance* and *desire*. This metaphor of our identity in Christ can be found widely in the Bible. Here's just two examples:

> Then I, John, saw the holy city, New Jerusalem, coming down out of heaven from God, *prepared as a bride adorned for her husband* (Revelation 21:2).

> Then one of the seven angels who had the seven bowls filled with the seven last plagues came to me and talked with me, saying, "Come, I will show you the bride, the Lamb's wife" (Revelation 21:9).

Imagery of a cosmic wedding starts in Genesis with Adam and Eve and ends in the Bible's final book. From cover to cover, the message is clear: *We're a bride that's being prepared for a great wedding at the end of this age. We'll be joined forever in affection to our Bridegroom, the Lord Jesus Christ.*

Believers fulfill the feminine role in our relationship with Jesus. He initiates, we respond; He gives, we receive; He impregnates, we bring to birth; He leads, we follow; He loves, we reciprocate; He rules, we reign with Him. This is not a feminized gospel but a recognition He's the stronger. Men forsake none of their masculinity in relating to Jesus as His bride, just as women forsake none of their femininity when they identify as sons of God (Luke 20:36). These metaphors are given, not to confine our identity, but to expand our understanding of who we are in Christ. No single metaphor captures our full identity. We're His temple, His body, His bride, His children, His sons, His army—and more! The dignity of who we are in Christ is just staggering.

Generally, sisters have an easier time than brothers with the secret of this chapter—learning to relate to Jesus as His lovesick bride. But the brothers can gain this secret, too. New dimensions of intimacy and responsiveness open to us when we connect to our bridal identity and relate to Jesus as our Bridegroom.

When Jesus looks at us, clothed in white, replete with good works, mature in affections, making ourselves ready for our wedding day, His ravished heart soars with delight. He's eagerly waiting for the day He marries His espoused virgin, and we can hardly wait, too! In the meantime, we court each other with love, attention, affection, honor, and desire. The secret place is the king's chamber where we nurture our growing love relationship (Song of Solomon 1:4).

This is where He washes us with words of affirmation, declaring how fair we are to Him. In response, we lavish Him with praise for His beauty, character, and power. In the secret place, as we receive His love, we're empowered to love Him with the same extravagance. He sure knows how to capture a heart and keep it!

Jesus didn't die to marry *amazon woman*—a battle axe of a bride that intimidates with her hulking strength and tough demeanor. Nor did He die to marry a workhorse who will tirelessly labor to fulfill His household chores and glean His fields. *He died for love.* He died for a beautiful bride who will walk with Him, talk with Him, dream with Him, laugh with Him, strategize with Him, and rule with Him.

When my bride came walking down the aisle toward me many years ago, with a white dress and glowing face, let me tell you what I *wasn't* thinking: *She's got good teeth. She bakes a mean pie. She'll do my laundry and prepare my meals. She'll change the kids' diapers. She'll keep the house clean.* Here's what I *was* thinking: *Here comes my lover!* Yes, when we got married, I knew Marci would manage our home, nurture our children, prepare meals, and do laundry; but that's not why we married. We got married for love.

We're getting married to Christ for love.

True, we're soldiers of Christ. We're involved in high-level strategic warfare, and the Lord calls us to fight the good fight of faith. And true, we're laborers in His vineyard. We work tirelessly in the harvest to bring all the wheat into His barn. But Jesus didn't die to enlist an army or a labor force; He died for a bride.

True, we come to the secret place to receive battle plans from the Commander-In-Chief. And true, we come to regain strength for the day's labors in the field. But that's not the primary role of the secret place. Above all, we come for intimacy. We come in our highest identity—as His bride—to enjoy His embrace and lavish Him with love.

In the Bible's last chapter, we hear the cry that will grip believers at the end of the age: "And the Spirit and the bride say, 'Come!' And let him who hears say, 'Come!' And let him who thirsts come. Whoever desires, let him take the water of life freely" (Revelation 22:17). At the end of the age, the church will stand in her identity as a *bride*. I believe this is a prophetic declaration that in these end times God's people are awaking to their identity as the bride of Christ. The bride will partner with the Spirit to prepare for the return of the Bridegroom.

A bride and bridegroom love to be together. Knowing that, let me ask a question. Do you ever waste time with the Lord? With that question, I'm thinking of Mary of Bethany who lavished her inheritance (the costly flask of fragrant oil) upon the Lord, and was rebuked by the disciples, *Why this waste?* (Matthew 26:8). They viewed her effusive display of love as wasteful. But Jesus validated her love, confirming that love is sometimes *wasteful* in its extravagance.

So again, do you ever waste time with your Beloved? What I mean is, after you've done your typical regimen in the secret place—Bible reading, praise, worship, petitions, intercession, praying in the Spirit—and once your time is finished, do you ever spend a little more hang time with Him just for love? I mean, why not? Stay a bit longer and *waste* some time in His presence—because you're a lovesick bride, and you just want to be with Him.

When we awaken to our bridal identity, spending time with Him ceases to feel like a duty, and becomes our soul's delight. When other tasks pull us away from that companionship, we actually feel frustrated. And then the feelings of anticipation for our next time together grow stronger.

The Lord wants to move our secret place from a religious obligation to a romantic adventure.

When John saw the bride of Christ in her glory, he saw her as *a city whose length, breadth, and height are equal* (Revelation 21:16). When Paul extolled Christ's love, he wrote about the *length, breadth, and height* of Christ's love (Ephesians 3:17-19). Same language. Both Bridegroom and bride have the same dimensions of love:

- Length: Even as Christ's love plunged to the depths of people's sin, this bride's love reaches down to the lowest specimens of humanity to lift them to glory. Nothing is spared to express the lengths of this love. She doesn't love her life, even unto death, for the sake of the gospel.
- Breadth: Even as Christ's love reaches across every strata and division of humanity to encompass people of every language, color, and background, the bride's love also touches all peoples. Her heart is enflamed to embrace every person for whom Christ died.
- Height: Here are the glorious heights of her perfected love—the unspotted affections of a dazzling bride for her Beloved who is exalted above every other name. The purity and glory of her passions rise as a majestic mountain of regal splendor.

Wow, don't they make an awesome pair? Together, clothed in stunning perfection, fully compatible and equally yoked together in every way, they're the love story of heaven. Forever.

CHAPTER FORTY-SEVEN

The Secret of Clinging

> I cling to Your testimonies; O LORD, do not put me to shame! (Psalm 119:31).

As the *weaker vessel*, one of the things we feel deeply as the bride of Christ is our helplessness and vulnerability apart from Him. When we're in trouble or hurting, we especially feel our need of Him and cling to Him like a lifesaver.

The psalmist testified that, "Unless Your law had been my delight, I would then have perished in my affliction" (Psalm 119:92). We cling to His word because without it we would perish. In tough times, the secret place is literally our survival.

Sometimes I'm especially clingy. I've wondered, *Lord, are you displeased that I'm clinging to you so desperately right now?* The answer has been, *No, I love it when you cling to Me with all your might. Without Me you can do nothing, even when you're feeling strong and capable. I love it when you realize you need Me more than your next breath.*

Sometimes my soul is blown about by winds of warfare that I don't even understand. If I knew where the sniper was that's taking shots at me, I might have an idea how to defend myself. But I don't know where the hits are coming from. That's when I remind myself of David's words, "My adversaries are all before You" (Psalm 69:19). He sees all my enemies, even when I don't. He knows exactly the source and nature of my warfare, and He knows my best way forward. This is why I cling to Him in prayer. When the shrapnel is flying, sometimes the only thing I know to do is wrap myself around Him, tremble with longing, and cling white-knuckled in desperate dependence.

I used to think Christian maturity meant we get stronger and stronger until we intimidate the legions of darkness with our faith and power. But the biblical image of maturity is different from that: "Who is this coming up from the wilderness, leaning upon her beloved?" (Song of Solomon 8:5). By the final chapter of Song of Solomon, the bride has been perfected in love through the wilderness and here's the most striking quality of her maturity: she's depending on her Beloved for every step.

The mark of maturity is not that we're able to stand taller and stronger on our own, but that we're dependent on Him in literally every area of life. Maturity means we cling more than ever.

When it's time for me to speak to a group of people from God's word, if I'm feeling strong and confident in my preparation, I've learned that it's easier to move right past what He wants to do. But when I'm wobbly in my soul and leaning hard on the Lord for help with every word, I tend to follow Him more closely. Sometimes I just stand before the people and teeter. And dig my fingernails into His arm. In my times of greatest weakness, when I expected the meeting to be a failure, I've often been surprised at how strongly the Lord has worked through weakness.

You don't mind so much clinging to Him in public when you've already been clinging to Him in private. In the secret place, we launch the day by putting a death grip on Him and never letting go.

The Lord said through Moses, "That you may love the LORD your God, that you may obey His voice, and that you may *cling* to Him, for He is your life and the length of your days" (Deuteronomy 30:20). But the Jewish leaders of Jesus' day—those positioned as builders in the kingdom—had lost their *clinginess* to God. When the chief cornerstone came to them, they rejected Him (Psalm 118:22). They had been trained to be capable builders for God but, despite their expertise, they rejected God's stone because of their confidence in their own opinions and assumptions. How tragic! They rejected the very thing they'd been crying out to God for (the Messiah).

I want to learn from their example. I don't want to become so confident in my training and experience that I lose my sense of leaning on Jesus for every breath, every move, every idea, every opinion.

It's interesting to observe that, after Jesus rose from the dead, He appeared first to Mary Magdalene. You see, Mary was the last one at the tomb on the day of His burial, and she was the first one at the tomb on the morning of His resurrection. When nobody else was there, she was. She was last to leave and first to return. As it turned out, Jesus revealed Himself first to the one who missed Him most.

When Mary recognized Him, she was overcome with joy and wrapped her arms around his feet. She had lost Him once and wasn't about to let that happen again. Jesus said to her, *Don't cling to Me, for I have not yet ascended to My Father* (John 20:17). He wasn't upset that she wanted to hold onto Him. He was simply meaning, *It's not time yet. I know the purity of your heart, Mary. You want to be joined to me in love, and we will be joined together in that way forever. But not yet. First, I must ascend to the Father. Our clinging relationship will not come into fullness until later, in the kingdom of God.*

In clinging to Jesus, Mary Magdalene represented the end-time bride of Christ. In these last days a bridal company is arising that is yearning for Him, looking for Him, peering into the darkness, lovesick with longing to see Him. Weeping. Watching. Waiting. This is the kind of bride Jesus is coming back for. And when He reveals Himself to her the second time, she will not be put off any longer. Even if He should try to say, *Don't cling to Me*, these arms will wrap around His feet and never let go. Holding to Him for dear life, we'll say, *We lost You once, Lord, and we're never letting You out of our grip again!*

He's coming back first to those who miss Him most. And we'll cling to Him forever in love.

But until that glorious day, I'll cling to Him every day in secret.

CHAPTER FORTY-EIGHT

The Secret of Walking with God

God wants a walking partner. That's what He had in the beginning with Adam and Eve when they went *walking in the garden in the cool of the day* (Genesis 3:8). They enjoyed a walking relationship that involved companionship, dialogue, intimacy, joint decision-making, mutual delight, and shared dominion.

The walk He had with Adam and Eve—He wants it with *you*, too. This explains why you're feeling drawn to a closer walk with Him.

My wife, Marci, loves to go walking with her friend, Wendy. They talk the whole time. Nonstop. The walk makes exercise fun and deepens their friendship. Jesus went on these kinds of walks with His disciples, and He still likes to walk with us today.

The secret place isn't the destination but the catalyst. It's intended to establish and strengthen our friendship with God so that, after our secret time is over, we continue to walk with Him the rest of the day. We don't want just an hour of sweet fellowship in the morning; we want a 24-hour walk, every day, in unbroken communion with our Friend.

After Adam, Enoch was next in the Bible to walk with God:

> After he begot Methuselah, *Enoch walked with God* three hundred years, and had sons and daughters. So all the days of Enoch were three hundred and sixty-five years. And *Enoch walked with God*; and he was not, for God took him (Genesis 5:22-24).

Even though men began to call on the name of the Lord in the early days (Genesis 4:26), Enoch was first to explore the tangible delights of walking with God. He found something even Adam didn't experience. He pressed into God until he learned how to commune with Him throughout every part of every day. When he found this walking relationship, the Lord responded by catching him up to heaven.

God didn't take him up to glory so that we'd be impressed with Enoch's piety. God wasn't saying to us, *If you'll be as spiritual as Enoch, I'll translate you to heaven, too.* God translated Enoch to heaven to underscore how much He loves to walk with people. I suppose Him saying, *Enoch was the first to walk with Me, so I decided to highlight His example by doing something extraordinary. I caught Him up to paradise to show how much I long to have a walking relationship with My friends.*

Imagine being Enoch and having, for 365 years, a growing relationship with God! One can only imagine what kind of intimacy Enoch experienced. Perhaps Enoch's heart longed so deeply for more that God grew weary of withholding Himself. Maybe He was thinking, *Enoch, your longing for Me is so real and pure, I don't want to say no to you anymore. I'm going to answer your prayer and show you My face. Come on up!*

God wants to awaken your desire to walk with Him just as Enoch did. Not that He plans to translate you to heaven; but He does want to reveal the beauty of His face to you. He'll do this, as you walk with Him, by opening the Scriptures to you. The Spirit of revelation (Ephesians 1:17) will reveal to you the light of the glory of God that's in the face of Christ (2 Corinthians 4:6).

It's significant that God waited until Enoch was 365 years old to take him. Not 360 or 364, but 365. Why? Obviously, because there are 365 days in a year. By taking him on year 365, God was sending a message: *I want to walk with people 365 days a year. 364 days a year won't do. I want to walk with you today, all day, every day. All year. Every year. For the rest of your lives.* Who would've thought the God of the universe would be *this* interested in *us*? Mindboggling!

To those who walk with Him, He confides secrets. The ancients before us experienced this. Noah walked with God (Genesis 6:9), so God told him about His plans to destroy the earth with a flood. Abraham walked with God (Genesis 24:40), so He confided His plans to destroy Sodom. Through Christ, we can explore the adventure of walking with God—perhaps even in a fuller way than Noah and Abraham because of the Spirit who has been given to us.

God wants to walk *with* us before He works *through* us. He'll even wait to do something until He finds the right man or woman with whom He can work. To put it bluntly, He works with His friends. He doesn't decide what He wants to do and then start looking for someone to use; He looks for a friend and, once He's got them, He decides what He wants to do. Once He finds a Noah, His options open up. He can do anything now. He can even drown the entire globe in a flood.

First on His list—find a friend to walk with.

When God has a Noah, He can do a flood. When He has a Joseph, He can give Pharaoh a dream. When He has a Moses, He can take His people through the sea. When He has an Elijah, He can send fire from heaven. When He has a Samuel, He can test Saul's heart. When He has a Jesus, He can save the world. O beloved, walk with God!

When God has a friend, divine activity accelerates. For example, look at Daniel. Things were fairly routine around Babylon until Daniel showed up. But when Babylon took captive a man who walked with God, everything got turned on its head. Heaven began to rumble. Nebuchadnezzar received dreams of historic proportions; men were preserved in a fiery furnace; the king lost his mind for seven years and then got it back again; a hand appeared and wrote on a wall; lions couldn't eat supper; and some of the most powerful revelations of end-time events were given. All these things took place because God had a man who walked with Him.

If you put a riding lawn mower in my garage, I assure you that I *will* use it! I would never let something that useful go to waste. God's the same way. If you're a fully prepared vessel, He *will* use you.

This is why He wants to walk with you—so He can prepare you for noble purposes. During those walks, He'll infuse humility, faithfulness, and loyalty. He'll keep walking with you until you qualify as a useful vessel.

Here's the secret: *The secret place is where we develop a walking relationship with God.* We grow a secret history with Him in private, and then He can decide how He wants to manifest it in public. Picture an iceberg. Only 10% of an iceberg can be seen on the surface. When we walk with God, 90% of our walk is never seen by others. Build the 90% and He'll reveal the 10%.

Jesus said He confides in His friends (John 15:15). If you want a walking and talking friendship with Him, you're welcome to offer this prayer:

Lord, I want to be Your confidant, loyal to death. I want to walk with You, talk with You, listen to You, understand Your heart, and partner with You here and now. Teach me to walk with You.

CHAPTER FORTY-NINE

The Secret of Buying Oil

Oil is a biblical metaphor for the presence and ministry of the Holy Spirit (1 Samuel 16:13). When the Bible speaks of oil in a lamp, often it's signifying that we're a lamp that burns for God and the Holy Spirit is our empowering fuel. When we're full of the indwelling Holy Spirit, He brings us to life and illuminates our hearts with His love and glory.

Jesus spoke of *buying oil.* He meant that we'll have to pay a price, in the secret place, if we're to be filled with the Holy Spirit. Prayer is costly. What's the price? Time and energy. How do we buy oil? By taking the time to be with the Lord and be renewed in His word and Spirit. It takes energy and effort to renew our oil reserves.

The idea of *buying oil* derives from Jesus' parable of the ten virgins. As you review the passage, notice how *oil* appears in the parable:

> Then the kingdom of heaven shall be likened to ten virgins who took their lamps and went out to meet the bridegroom. Now five of them were wise, and five were foolish. Those who were foolish took their lamps and took no oil with them, but the wise took oil in their vessels with their lamps. But while the bridegroom was delayed, they all slumbered and slept. And at midnight a cry was heard: "Behold, the bridegroom is coming; go out to meet him!" Then all those virgins arose and trimmed their lamps. And the foolish said to the wise, "Give us some of your oil, for our lamps are going out." But the wise answered, saying, "No, lest there should not be enough for us and you; but go rather to those who sell, and buy for yourselves." And while they went to buy, the bridegroom came, and those who were ready went in with him to the wedding; and the door was shut. Afterward the other virgins came also, saying, "Lord, Lord, open to us!" But he answered and

> said, "Assuredly, I say to you, I do not know you." Watch therefore, for you know neither the day nor the hour in which the Son of Man is coming (Matthew 25:1-13).

When Jesus spoke of us having oil in our lamps, most interpreters agree He was meaning that we should have within an ample supply of the Holy Spirit. The focus is on getting oil. We want to be filled with the oil of the Holy Spirit so we can live an overcoming life in Christ and survive the chaos and calamities of these last days.

All the virgins had oil in their lamps, but the wise brought an extra vessel of oil with them. The foolish assumed the bridegroom's return would be sooner rather than later. Therefore, they exerted minimal effort to prepare themselves for his coming. They sincerely believed they had enough oil to sustain them until his arrival. In contrast, the wise had anticipated that the return of the bridegroom could be delayed longer than they expected.

Wisdom prepares a secret place for the long haul.

All ten were virgins, which is to say they were all sincere believers. Some see the virgins representing *leaders* in the body of Christ. According to that interpretation, the oil could represent a leader's ministry anointing that's cultivated in the secret place. The foolish virgins were leaders who got enough oil to *get by*. They invested in the secret place as much as seemed necessary to fulfill their ministry responsibilities. But the wise went beyond that. Yes, they wanted enough oil for ministry; but they also wanted sufficient oil to carry their hearts for the duration. Wise leaders always pursue a depth in God that goes beyond their ministry demands. They come to the secret place, not only to buy oil for ministry impartation, but also to buy oil for a personal, burning-heart relationship with Jesus.

Getting oil for ministry is costly, but not as costly as the oil of an intimate, passionate life with Jesus. Getting oil for ministry might require a 60-minute supply; oil for a burning heart requires a 24/7 supply.

We're being foolish when we keep our reserves quarter-full. It's foolish to allow the loud noises of the urgent to pull us away from that which is truly important—buying oil in the secret place. Don't settle for a minimal filling. Stay at His feet until your heart is brimming with love and faith.

When their foolishness became obvious, the foolish virgins turned to the wise and said, *Give us some of your oil*. They recognized the wise had cultivated, through time and energy, a greater depth in God. They were saying, *Give us some of your authority in ministry*. But the wise were helpless to give it. There simply are no shortcuts to carrying Holy Spirit oil. We can't borrow authority for ministry from other people; we can only buy it for ourselves—in the secret place.

Proverbs 13:12 says *hope deferred makes the heart sick*. When the bridegroom delayed his return, the hopes of the virgins were deferred and they were overtaken with heartsickness. Heartsickness had caused them to fall sleep from sorrow (Luke 22:45). All ten fell asleep from sorrow, but only half had the reserves to recover. The bridegroom's delay served to distinguish the wise from the foolish. In other words, the delay revealed those who had developed the carrying power of a personal history with the bridegroom.

Proverbs 13:12 goes on to say that *when the desire comes, it's a tree of life*. Holy desires, finally fulfilled, become a tree of life to feed a generation. In our parable, the virgins' desire was for the coming of the bridegroom. Those who persevered in love through the heartsickness found the bridegroom's coming to be a tree of life. Their faithfulness became a source of life for their generation.

To sustain in the hour of trial that's coming on the earth (Revelation 3:10), we must cultivate oil reserves in the Holy Spirit. That's the point of the parable—buy oil! Devote yourself to the secret place until your heart is overflowing with love and desire for your Beloved. Then, make oil replenishment the first priority of each day. This chapter's secret is tucked away right here: The secret place is the threshold for the infilling we need to sustain through the dark night of Christ's delays.

Buy oil!

CHAPTER FIFTY

The Secret of Constant Supply

We have access, by God's grace, to a ceaseless supply of the Holy Spirit. We need never be depleted spiritually because He's More-Than-Enough. We simply learn to tap into the Spirit's resources. The secret place is our lab where we learn to draw more and more on His grace, and then live each day in the strength of His endless supply.

We're going to look at the vision of Zechariah 4 as a picture of how to draw on the Spirit's *constant supply*. Please find Zechariah 4 in your Bible right now and read it first so you can follow the content of this chapter.

Zechariah saw a lampstand with seven oil-fed lamps. Above the lampstand was a bowl filled with oil, with pipes leading down from the bowl to each lamp. The bowl was an oil reservoir, and was fed by two olive trees which stood at the lampstand's left and right. The olive trees dripped oil constantly, and two pipes channeled the oil from the trees to the bowl. The trees supplied the bowl, and the bowl supplied the lamps. The flow was constant, and the flames of the lamps burned incessantly.

There are at least four biblical ways to interpret the lampstand of Zechariah 4. My favorite of the four is to see the lampstand as representing *you* and *me*—the Lord's servant.

Who was the Lord's servant in Zechariah's vision? Jerusalem's leader at the time—Zerubbabel. Now consider Revelation 11, which is the sister passage to Zechariah 4. Who was the Lord's servant in Revelation 11:3-4? The two witnesses in the end times. In both visions, the Lord's servants were described as *lampstands*. Both visions infer that God wants His servants to burn before Him as seven-flamed lampstands. The lampstand of Zechariah 4, therefore, represents *you* (the Lord's servant).

Initially, I didn't see the lampstand as representing a person because I thought a believer had only one fire burning within. But then I came across Jesus' exhortation, "Let your waist be girded and your lamps burning" (Luke 12:35). Jesus spoke of *lamps* (plural), indicating that we have multiple lamps within.

How many lamps do we have? I find a hint in Revelation 4:5, where the Holy Spirit is revealed as seven Spirits that burn as *seven lamps of fire* before the throne. When we're filled with that Holy Spirit, His seven lamps ignite our lamps. Therefore, I believe we also have seven lamps. We have the potential of burning with the same seven fires that kindle the Holy Spirit.

What are the seven fires of the Holy Spirit? If I knew, perhaps I could more easily catch their flame. But I don't know their identity because the Scriptures are rather obscure here. I wonder, though, if the foremost lamp of the Holy Spirit might be *the fire of God's love*. This much I know—God has a fiery love for the people He created. When that fire grips our lives, it will set us ablaze with passion for Jesus and compassion for people. I want the fire of His love burning in my heart!

What are the other six fires of the Holy Spirit? I have only theories, I really don't know for sure. But whatever the identity of the Holy Spirit's seven fires, *I want to be kindled with all seven!* I believe the secret place is where we catch these fires.

Now to the historical background of Zechariah's vision. Zerubbabel, Israel's civic leader, was tasked with building God's temple but needed encouragement. The message of Zechariah's vision was intended to strengthen Zerubbabel's hands by showing him a new paradigm of how to build in the kingdom. Most kingdom building is done by visionary leaders who mobilize a group of people to use their strengths to hammer away at a project until it's finished. But God wanted Zerubbabel to learn another kind of leadership—a style of leadership in which His servant derives their effectiveness by drawing upon an inner source in the Spirit.

When ignited on the inside by a constant supply of the Spirit, a leader is empowered more effectively to lead God's people in the building of the kingdom. Instead of being shown a leader who was spread thin by running in a thousand directions at once, in his vision Zechariah saw a leader whose lamps were burning brightly because they were drawing upon a spiritual source of power and grace. This kind of leader doesn't build by human might or power, "'But by My Spirit,' says the LORD of hosts" (Zechariah 4:6).

The bowl holding the oil was said to be *above* the lampstand. The oil flowed *down* from the bowl into the seven lamps. The bowl supplied each lamp with *gravity-fed pressure.* With oil pressing into each lamp, the flames burned brightly—veritable torches of holy zeal. God was showing Zechariah that it's possible to access such a dynamic flow of divine life that one literally burns with fiery zeal before God and His people.

Place yourself in this vision and see yourself as a lampstand. You're called to provide compassionate leadership to others as you build together in the kingdom of God. You want to be a leader like Zerubbabel who comes aside into the secret place, opens the channels of your heart, and allows the oil of the Holy Spirit to fuel every flame of your heart. The secret place is where your lamps are trimmed and where your zeal for the face of Jesus is renewed until you burn with seven bright, torch-like flames.

May you so burn for Christ that everyone you contact is impacted with your passion for Jesus and your selfless love for people. Your fire is hot and your flame is pure. You're seared clean from self-serving ambitions and personal agendas. Your heart is enthralled with the beauty of your King. Your interests and affections are for nothing other than your heavenly Bridegroom. When you sound a call to build, the saints rally around the vision because they know you're functioning from the creative womb of the morning. You're leading, not from humanly manufactured dreams, but from divinely downloaded mandates and insights. Your productivity becomes disproportionate to your resources.

The work accelerates forward at a pace faster than seems possible with your limited resources. Why? Because you're not just working by the might and power of human resources; you're operating in the synergy and flow of Holy Spirit momentum as God works with and in you. You've found the secret! Financial resources come out of seemingly nowhere; volunteers come out of the proverbial woodwork; secular corporations start donating their stuff to you; doors open where only a wall existed; saints are joined together in kingdom purpose; unbelievers are amazed at the grace of God that rests upon the community of believers. And it was all unlocked because a servant leader came out of the secret place on fire for God.

While receiving the vision, Zechariah had one nagging question of his angelic guide. Three times in chapter 4, Zechariah asked the angel, *Tell me about those two olive trees. What are the olive trees?* (see Zechariah 4:4, 11, and 12). The angel's answers were elusive and obscure: "These are the two anointed ones, who stand beside the Lord of the whole earth" (Zechariah 4:14).

Zechariah wanted to know the identity of the two olive trees because they were the *source* of the oil. If he knew the source of the Spirit's oil, he'd know the secret of living in a constant supply of divine life and grace. So this really is the great question of all time. What is the source for a never-ending supply of God's infinite resources?

If the lampstand represents Zerubbabel, let me suggest the two olive trees represent *the word and the Spirit*. We need both the word and Spirit, mixed together and flowing into our hearts, if we're to build the kingdom through the power of God. When the Spirit of God illumines us with revelation from His word, we come alive with holy fire!

That's what happened to the two disciples on the road to

Emmaus. Jesus opened their understanding in the Scriptures concerning Himself. This was Jesus revealing Jesus to the human spirit through the power of the Holy Spirit—lifechanging! The disciples later declared, "Did not our heart burn within us while He talked with us on the road, and while He opened the Scriptures to us?" (Luke 24:32).

When the Spirit mixes with the word and sends that oil to your lamps, your heart will burn for Jesus, too!

The secret place is where we meditate in the word until the Spirit mixes with it and sets our lamps ablaze. When this admixture of oil (word and Spirit) flows into our hearts and ignites our fire, the kingdom will advance in fruitfulness beyond all expectations.

The issue is not, *Work harder.* The issue is, *Get oil.* Here's the secret. Devote yourself to enlarging your connection to the source of divine oil. The more His holy oil flows into your inner being, the brighter your lamps will shine before God and men.

The powers of darkness in a region are pushed back on their heels when a man or woman finds the unceasing wellspring of heaven's life in the secret place. When they're fed from an inner oil source and their lamps are torches of zeal for their Beloved, no force of hell can douse this flame. Even if the dragon tries to extinguish it with a flood from his mouth, it's fed by an internal source. Nothing external can quench it. John Wesley said it something like this, *Get on fire for God and people will come to watch you burn.*

CHAPTER FIFTY-ONE

The Secret of Abiding in Christ

There's one great question that the luminaries of sacred history have asked as they've pursued God. This question was asked *three times* by Zechariah in the passage we examined in chapter 50. It's the common quest of every diligent seeker—the soul's supreme search. It can be expressed many ways but is distilled to this: *How do I abide in Christ?* What a question!

All of us ache with this same reach. We want unbroken intimacy, a 24/7 abiding relationship with Jesus. But how do we find it? It feels like a moving target. If we start the morning connected to Him, by afternoon it can feel like a distant memory. Close, then far. In, then out. Then close again. Then distant again. And we hate it. The roller coast ride drives us crazy on the inside. Does it have to be this way?

An abiding relationship with Christ is the common longing of every noble heart.

When Jesus extended His call to abide in Him, He gave us one of the most hopeful promises of the entire Bible: "If you abide in Me, and My words abide in you, you will ask what you desire, and it shall be done for you. By this My Father is glorified, that you bear much fruit; so you will be My disciples" (John 15:7-8). The *if* of the passage almost drives us insane with holy desire. If! *The great condition to answered prayer is an abiding relationship with Christ.*

We know this close a relationship is available, and yet it seems elusive. We want it to be so real, so tangible, that He answers all our prayers. Have you attained a place in Christ where all your prayers are answered? I haven't. But I'm not giving up. I've climbed too far on the mountain to give up now. Instead, I'm going to ramp up my search. I've got *holy heartburn*—my spiritual appetite for the things of Christ is only growing. I must gain Christ!

Hudson Taylor wrote of his struggles to find a closer walk with God. Although he's considered one of history's greatest missionaries, he longed for a more intimate relationship with Christ. "I prayed, agonized, fasted, strove, made resolutions, read the word more diligently, sought more time for retirement and meditation—but all was without effect," he pined. "I knew that if I would abide in Christ all would be well, but I could not." Taylor reached a turning point in his life when he received a letter from a colleague with this message: *Friendship with God comes not from striving after faith but from resting in the faithful one.* Those simple words unlocked something and helped him cross a threshold in his relationship with Jesus. He was able to cease striving and embrace Christ's nearness, power, and life. Yes, even a champion like Hudson Taylor wrestled to abide in Christ.

The way you come to abide in Him will be different from others. We all abide differently because we're all uniquely fashioned by God. Your relationship with Christ will never be like mine, and mine will never be like yours. That's why you won't learn to abide in Christ by gleaning others' stories. It won't come by reading the right book or hearing the right sermon. No one can mentor you into an abiding relationship with Christ. A mentor might be able to lay out some of the ground rules, but in the final analysis each of us must find our own way to abiding. When all is said and done, we must shut the door, get into the secret place with Christ, and discover what an abiding relationship with Him looks like for ourselves.

Jesus gave us a Helper in this quest—the Holy Spirit. You don't need anyone to help you with the Helper. Just go to the Helper and ask Him to guide you into this abiding reality.

Often the journey to an abiding relationship with Christ is attended by duress. God will design distressing circumstances in our lives to press us more desperately into Him. In His kindness, He'll interrupt our lives to guide us into the kind of relationship we've always wanted but didn't know how to find.

Joseph is a perfect example of this. God took him on a painful pathway in order to help him find an abiding relationship. Here's how it happened.

As a 17-year-old, Joseph stood apart from his brothers as a man of godly character. Seeing his consecration, God basically said, *Congratulations, Joseph, for keeping your heart pure. You're walking blamelessly before Me and keeping yourself separate from an evil generation. You've qualified for a promotion in the kingdom—to slavery you go!* So Joseph was sold into slavery by his brothers.

In Egypt, he was bought by a man named Potiphar. Potiphar soon realized God blessed everything Joseph touched, so he appointed him chief steward of all his business dealings. Joseph was careful in His walk before God and he kept passing His pop quizzes. He was diligent and faithful to cultivate his gifts and talents. He fled from sexual temptation when Potiphar's wife tried to seduce him. God basically responded with, *Congratulations, Joseph, you're continuing to practice My presence. You've faithfully cultivated your talents, and you've fled temptation. You've qualified for another promotion in the kingdom—to prison you go!*

Joseph was in God's promotion system.

He had no idea why God allowed him to be thrown into prison. I wonder if he was tempted to think, *God, what's the use of serving You? When I love and serve You and keep a guard over my heart, it does no good.* Satan wanted to convince Joseph that serving God didn't pay. But Joseph guarded his heart and set his affections on his God.

Prison made Joseph desperate. He realized that, apart from divine intervention, he would spend the rest of his life rotting in that Egyptian prison. None of his talents were working for him here. It didn't matter that he was gifted and charismatic and brilliant; none of those talents could get him out of prison. Every gift he had cultivated in Potiphar's house was now useless. Hopelessly incarcerated, Joseph began to cry out to God with intense desperation. *God, talk to me, or my life is over!* He began to push roots down into the Spirit of God deeper than ever before. *God, why have you allowed this to happen to me? Why is nothing about my faith working for me right now?*

The Spirit just seemed to say, *Deeper*, so he kept reaching deeper into the heart of God. *Still deeper*. In desperation, Joseph pressed into the depths of the Spirit of God. *Go deeper, Joseph*. Prayerfully, he kept extending his spiritual roots deeper and deeper into the Spirit of God.

One day I believe he found the river. There is a river in God that runs so deep, we rarely find it apart from extraordinary motivation. God used the duress of prison to motivate Joseph to go after this river. When he found it, he discovered there's a source in God that runs deeper than the seasons of life. Winter or summer, flood or drought, it doesn't matter. Find the river and you access a wellspring of divine life that is unfazed by the four seasons. Few seem to find it, but when they do, they call it *abiding in Christ*.

God was essentially saying to Joseph, *Son, I have great things in store for you. But this calling will never be managed by the strength of your gifts and talents. As long as your strengths are intact, you'll always default to them. To train your spirit, I'm going to put you in a place where your strengths will be useless—prison.* When helpless and out of control, that's where he discovered a dimension in God that is *not by might, nor by power, but by the Spirit of the Lord* (Zechariah 4:6).

It was Joseph's ability to tap into the river of the Spirit that got him out of prison. His talents couldn't pull off a prison break, but his life in the Spirit could. When Pharaoh called on him to interpret his dream, Joseph delivered season-shifting wisdom because the Spirit was resting on him. In one hour,

He went from prison to palace.

Epochs and seasons change when we abide in Christ. We find the God zone—the dimension where God works mightily in the affairs of men. Joseph, the prophets, Jesus, Paul—they changed our planet's history by abiding in the secret place of the Most High. They've shown us the way. Find that same internal river of *abiding in Christ* and you'll impact your generation for God, too.

Don't be discouraged by the hardship that has suddenly accosted you. Press into God like never before. Turn desperation into abandonment. The secret is this: If you'll seek Him with all your heart, He'll guide you to the ancient river that runs deep in His heart. Here flow the clear waters of divine life. When the life of God touches your world of impossibilities, this is the stuff of miracles. Nothing stops the life of God. No prison, no wall, no mountain, no authority. The movements of the Spirit are unstoppable and the word of God can't be chained (2 Timothy 2:9). Drink of this river and everything in your world will shake and shudder under the groundswell of God's power. *You will ask what you desire, and it shall be done for you* (John 15:7).

Hear it again: *Learn to abide in Christ!*

CHAPTER FIFTY-TWO

The Secret of Union with God

Implanted in the human soul is a profoundly deep longing for a heart connection with God. We want to be joined to God in a way that's personal, identifiable, and *real.* It's your cry for intimacy with God that has driven you to read this book all the way to the last chapter. This same desire to connect with God filled the heart of the Samaritan woman in John 4. She had looked for love in all the wrong places, but the Master knew her sinful lifestyle proceeded from a longing to love and be loved. He came to her with redemption.

As Jesus' conversation with her progressed, she suddenly realized He was a prophet, so she immediately went to the great controversy between Jews and Samaritans: *Where is the right place to connect with God?* This was her nagging question: "Our fathers worshiped on this mountain, and you Jews say that in Jerusalem is the place where one ought to worship" (John 4:20). She wanted to know, *What's the right way to connect with God—here on this mountain or in Jerusalem?*

She had been told that connecting with God was an issue of *where.* Location. Place. If she had to go to Jerusalem to connect with God, her hopes would be miserably buried because she wasn't permitted (as a Samaritan) to enter Jerusalem's temple. Perhaps her lifestyle of sin sprang from a sense of hopelessness—despairing that she could ever connect with God. But in spite of her despair, her heart still ached to know God.

Jesus' response must have amazed her. He was suggesting that closeness to God was not a matter of physical location but of spirit connection. He said that, although she was seeking to connect with God, He was even more eagerly interested in connecting with her. He told her the Father is *seeking.*

He's seeking those who will connect with Him in Spirit and truth (John 4:23). Jesus sought her out to reveal the Father's desire for *her.*

It's about as unthinkable to us today as it was to her back then: The Father *desires* worshipers like you and me. He wants to be joined to us in love.

Who could have guessed this? He longs to be one with us, to have one heartbeat with us.

The ancients used the term *union with God* to describe the highest dimensions of spiritual intimacy. This is the connection with God for which the human heart burns. Jesus came to make us one with God (John 17:21-23). The greatest exhilaration of the human soul is found through union with God. This is where we discover and explore the cavernous depths of God's burning heart.

God created us with a desire for union with Him, and then helped us understand that longing by giving us the metaphor of marriage. Just as a husband and wife are joined as one, we are joined in union with God. This was Paul's primary point in Ephesians 5. First, he quoted Moses: "For this reason a man shall leave his father and mother and be joined to his wife, and the two shall become one flesh" (Ephesians 5:31). Then he added this comment: "This is a great mystery, but I speak concerning Christ and the church" (Ephesians 5:32). Like a husband and wife, Christ and the church are joined together in spiritual union.

Now, why do a young man and woman choose to marry? Is it for romance? Well, a couple can enjoy the romance of courtship without getting married (I speak of courtship in its purity and innocence). They can have love, intimacy, friendship, companionship, communication, and fellowship without getting married. If an unmarried couple can enjoy all those benefits, then why get married? Because there's one thing that courtship, in its purity, doesn't provide: *Union.*

Couples get married for *union.*

We've been made by God to desire union with a spouse, but even more than that, with *Him*. We're keenly anticipating the day when we'll be joined to Christ at the marriage supper of the Lamb (Revelation 19:9). In that day, we'll enjoy complete union with Christ. In the meantime, we can access limited dimensions of union with Him here on earth. To what degree can we be joined to Christ now? We're all pressing in to discover the answer.

There's one verse, above all others, that has inspired me in my pursuit of union with God. It's tucked away quietly in a somewhat obscure passage, but one day it caught me: "But he who is joined to the Lord is one spirit with Him" (1 Corinthians 6:17). In context, Paul was speaking of the union that happens through sexual relations (such as in prostitution). His inference was that sexual union somehow points to a kind of spiritual union we have with Christ which far surpasses the physical/sexual plane.

Here's what grabbed me about the verse. It says the Lord and I are *one spirit*. When I envisioned spiritual communion with Him, I always pictured two separate spirits, as though His Spirit and mine were kissing. But this Scripture reveals that when we're joined to Christ, we're no longer two spirits but one. *One spirit with God!* The idea is simply *fantastic*, bordering almost on the preposterous. It's almost too good to be true. *When I surrender to Christ, the two of us become one.*

The highest heavens can't contain God (Acts 7:49-50), but somehow He's ordained the human soul to become His habitation. That means our soul is broader in its ability to contain God than the entire universe. Truly we are fearfully and wonderfully made! We're capable of *being filled with all the fullness of God* (Ephesians 3:19). Wow. Little wonder that Christ in me is called *the hope of glory* (Colossians 1:27).

Let me illustrate this oneness with a question. If I were to pour a cup of pure water into the ocean, would you say the ocean is now diluted? No, you would say that cup of water has been absorbed and lost in the vastness of the ocean. That's what happens in union with Christ. When I'm joined to Him, I lose myself in the ocean of His greatness. Now I can say, "It is no longer I who live, but Christ lives in me" (Galatians 2:20). When I'm one with Him, my identity is gloriously lost in the immensity of His majesty and splendor.

I'm not suggesting that we become God. Far from it. We are eternally the created, and He is eternally the Creator. The distinction between Creator and created will never blur. But in some glorious way, the creature becomes one spirit with the Creator. We're joined together in eternal affection and devotion.

If our union with Christ seems mindboggling to you, imagine how dumbfounded it must leave the angels. From eternity past, they've witnessed a fiery furnace of love that has been limited to only Three Persons—Father, Son, and Holy Spirit. These Three have enjoyed an affection of astronomical proportions that is so fiery in intensity and scope that no other creature has ever dared step into that blazing furnace. In this eternal inferno of everlasting love, the Father's heart is joined to His Son, the Son is drawn into the depths of the Spirit, and the Spirit burns in the heart of the Father. Three in One! And now, as the angels gaze into this fiery furnace, they see the form of a fourth walking in the fire (Daniel 3:25). And this fourth person has the appearance of the bride of Christ!

Yes, it's true. Fallen humanity has been elevated to oneness with the Godhead. We've been invited into the love circle of the Trinity. The full ramifications are beyond comprehension to even the brilliant seraphim who blaze inside God's throne.

For now, what does it mean to be *joined to Christ*? How do we attain this? One way we pursue this is expressed by David in Psalm 63:8, "My soul *follows close* behind You." The Hebrew word for *follows close* is related to the word *joined*. To follow close is *to pursue with the intent to overtake*. David was saying, *Lord, I'm pursuing closely behind You with the objective of overtaking You. And when I do, I'll lay hold of You and never let You go! When I wrap my arms around You, I'll be joined to You forever.*

To be joined to Christ, therefore, is to chase after Him intensely with the intent of laying hold of Him. This magnificent obsession of the secret place is the holy chase to which we've been invited.

When I think of being joined to Christ, I'm reminded of Mary Magdalene's story. She loved Jesus in a special way because He had cast seven demons out of her and released her from her torment. The way she loved was demonstrated at Christ's death and resurrection. When Jesus was buried, she was the last one to sit and weep at His tomb before Sabbath's nightfall. And on resurrection morning, she was the first one to return to His tomb. How she loved Him! Then, when Jesus revealed Himself to her at the tomb, she instantly wrapped her arms around His feet and clung to Him in love. She didn't want to be separated ever again.

Jesus revealed Himself first to the one who loved Him most.

Mary represents the end-time bride of Christ. Like her, we're pursuing Him because of our longing to be joined to Him. Here we stand, at the end of the ages, yearning for His appearing. Like Mary at the tomb, we're looking, weeping, longing, yearning, watching. Our prayer echoes Mary's at the tomb: *Heavenly Father, where have You carried Him away? Bring Him here to me and I'll be satisfied, because I long to be with Him.*

When Jesus returns, He's going to reveal Himself first to His bride who longs for Him most.

When He comes the second time, and we see the one for whom our soul longs, we'll lay hold of Him, wrap our arms around Him, and this time *we'll never let go.*

He will "transform our lowly body that it may be conformed to His glorious body" (Philippians 3:21). The

Bridegroom and His perfected Bride will walk the aisle of Glory together and be joined in holy matrimony, the Father of lights officiating. Nothing will ever separate us again. No more crying, no more pain, no more tears. The Desire of the Nations will be fulfilled. And so we will ever be with the Lord.

But until then, I will retreat to my secret place, a heartsick, lovesick bride who longs to behold her Bridegroom. I'll pursue Him until I overtake Him. And I'll thrill in our quiet secret—the place of highest intimacy—for here I am joined to Him and we are one spirit.

Secrets of the Secret Place Curriculum

Bob Sorge's Secret Place Curriculum consists of four materials:

1. *Secrets of the Secret Place*
   The book you're holding is one of the leading resources in the world for helping believers establish a secret place relationship with Jesus. Use this book in small groups, training institutes, colleges, and local churches. Available in both paperback and hardcover.

2. *Companion Study Guide*
   The *Secrets of the Secret Place Companion Study Guide* is useful for both private and group study. Discussion questions help a group engage with the content of each chapter. Many in the group will want to get their own copy.

3. *Secrets Video Course*
   The secret place video course, taught by Bob, consists of twelve 30-minute sessions. This video series adds interest to a group study and strengthens the message of the book. The series can be purchased in DVD format, or streamed for free on YouTube—see Bob Sorge's Channel on YouTube.

4. *Leader's Manual*
   Almost anyone can lead a group through the Secrets Video Series simply by using the *Leader's Manual.* You'll receive guidelines for leading the group, along with handouts for each person. Photocopy and distribute the handouts for each person to complete while watching the film. The *Leader's Manual* is available in booklet form, or may be downloaded on the *Free Downloads* page at www.oasishouse.com.

This Secret Place Curriculum is an unparalleled tool for equipping believers in the necessity and magnificence of a secret place relationship with Jesus. Get your small group onto this!

Books by Bob Sorge

Secrets Curriculum

- *Secrets of the Secret Place* (paperback & hardcover)
- *Secrets of the Secret Place: Companion Study Guide*
- Secrets 12-part Video Series
- Leaders Manual

Prayer

Reset: 20 Ways to a Consistent Prayer Life
Unrelenting Prayer
Illegal Prayers
Power of the Blood
Minute Meditations

Worship

Exploring Worship: A Practical Guide to Praise and Worship
Glory: When Heaven Invades Earth
Following The River: A Vision For Corporate Worship

Enduring Faith

In His Face
The Fire Of Delayed Answers
The Fire Of God's Love
Pain, Perplexity, & Promotion: A Prophetic Interpretation of the Book of Job
Opened From the Inside: Taking the Stronghold of Zion
God's Still Writing Your Story
The Chastening of the Lord: The Forgotten Doctrine

Leadership
Dealing With the Rejection and Praise of Man
Envy: The Enemy Within
Loyalty: The Reach Of The Noble Heart
It's Not Business It's Personal
A Covenant With My Eyes
Stuck: Help for the Troubled Home

For info on each title, go to oasishouse.com.

Bob's books are available at:

- Oasis House, 816-767-8880
- oasishouse.com
- christianbook.com
- amazon.com
- Kindle, iBooks, Nook, Google Play
- Audible

To stay connected:
YouTube/bobsorge
Instagram: bob.sorge
Blog: bobsorge.com
twitter.com/BOBSORGE
Facebook.com/BobSorgeMinistry

Another powerful Secret Place book:

A 20-day guide that helps believers become established in the building blocks of a consistent prayer life. If *Secrets* inspires you to pray, *Reset* gives the practical how-to tools to make it work every day. Only 80 pages.

Consider using *Reset* for

- Church-wide prayer initiatives
- Discipling new believers
- Small group studies

Check out PrayerReset.com for amazing quantity discounts so entire congregations can do this book together. Available in several languages.

PrayerReset.com